READWELL'S

LEARN TELUGU

IN A MONTH

Easy Method of Learning Telugu
Through English Without a Teacher

Govindarajulu
B.A., D.B.M.

Readwell Publications
NEW DELHI-110008

Published by :
READWELL PUBLICATIONS
B-8, Rattan Jyoti, 18, Rajendra Place
New Delhi-110 008 (INDIA)
Phone : 5737448, 5712649, 5721761
Fax : 91-11-5812385
E-mail : readwell@sify.com
newlight@vsnl.net

ISBN 81-87782-08-0

Printed at : Arya Offset Press, New Delhi.

Preface

Language is only medium of intimate and effective communication. Two persons knowing no common language are just like two statues facing each other, looking at each other but not developing any intimacy. So every one must know a few languages so that their understanding of the people may help them to demolish regional and language barriers.

This book is the beginner's password for entering the citadel of language. It will help to learn an unknown language right from the alphabet through a known language. Learning a language through translation is like wooing a lady through an attorney, says Tagore. We have adopted a practical method.

—Author

CONTENTS

There are authors who choose to teach a language through the medium of translation. Their method is to compile a few hundred sentences, generally spoken on various occasions, categorise them and present them to the learner in the fond belief that he needs to learn only this much. The grammatical aspect of the language is ignored. In our view this method is inadequate. The learner cannot form sentences of his own because of the lack of knowledge of the rudiments of grammar. We have, therefore, chosen to teach grammar also so that the learner catches the language at the grassroots level and acquires self-confidence.

Although great care has been taken to prepare this book, yet there may be shortcomings in it. We are open to valuable suggestions and constructive criticism in our firm belief that we provide the maximum benefit to the learner.

How to Write

VOWELS

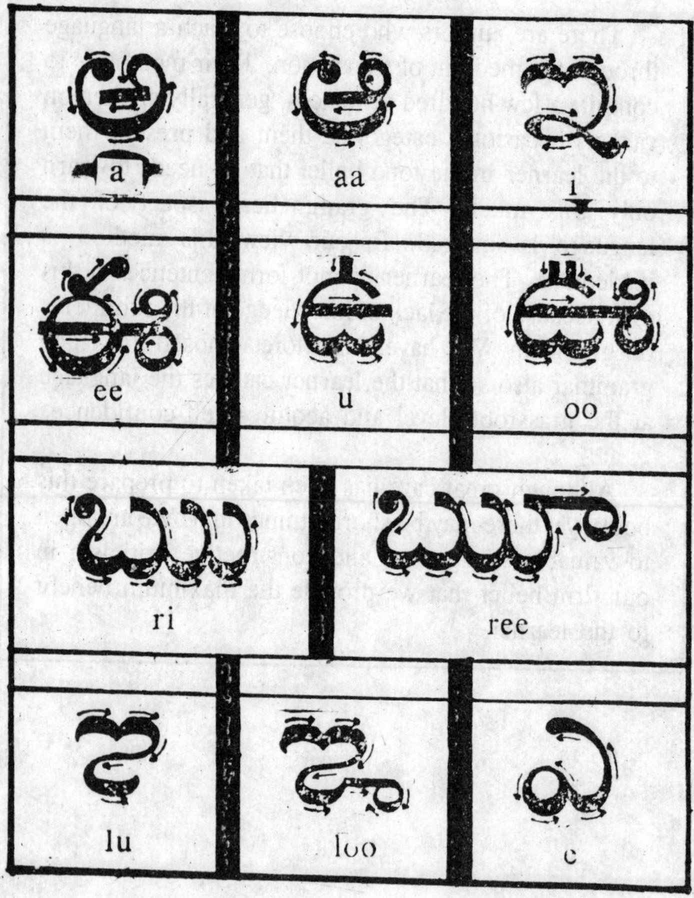

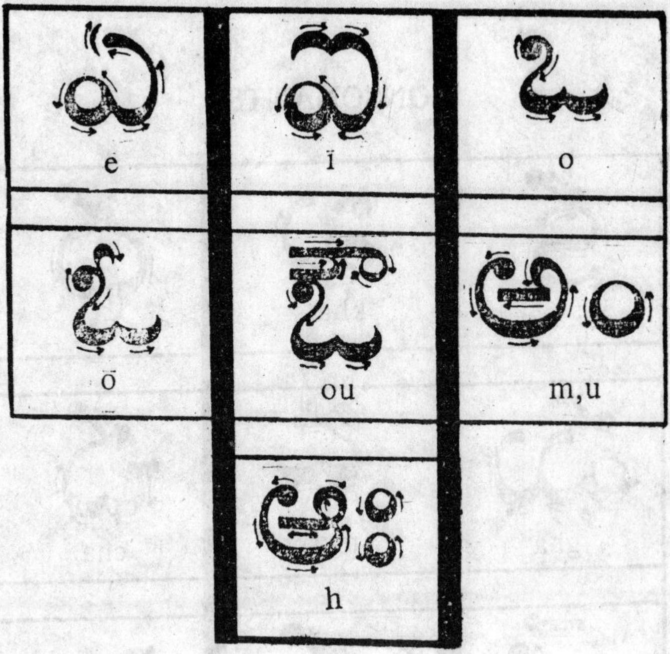
e
ī
o
ō
ou
m,u
h

CONSONANTS

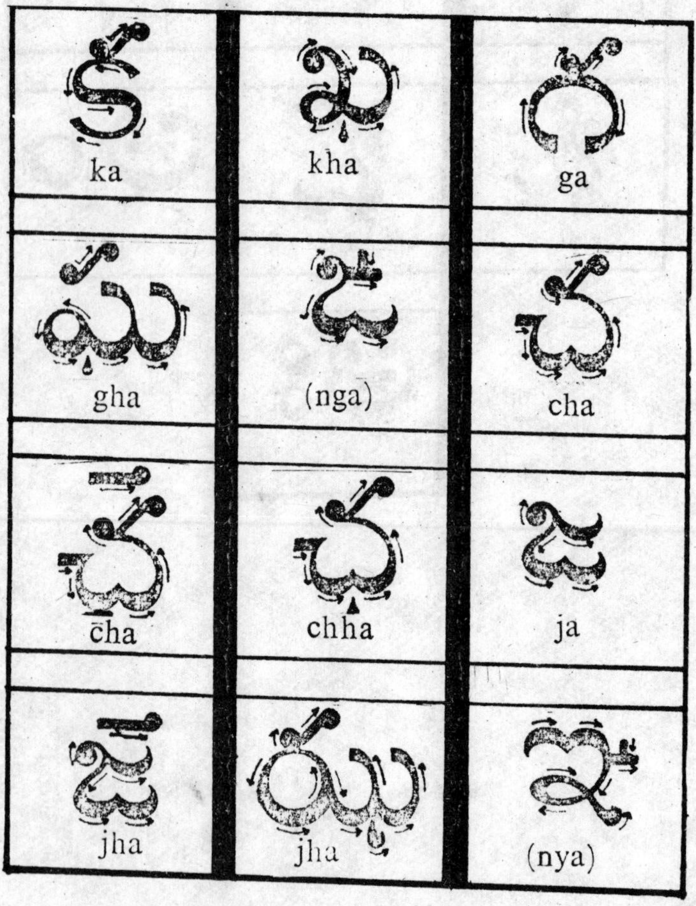
ka
kha
ga
gha
(nga)
cha
c̄ha
chha
ja
jha
jha
(nya)

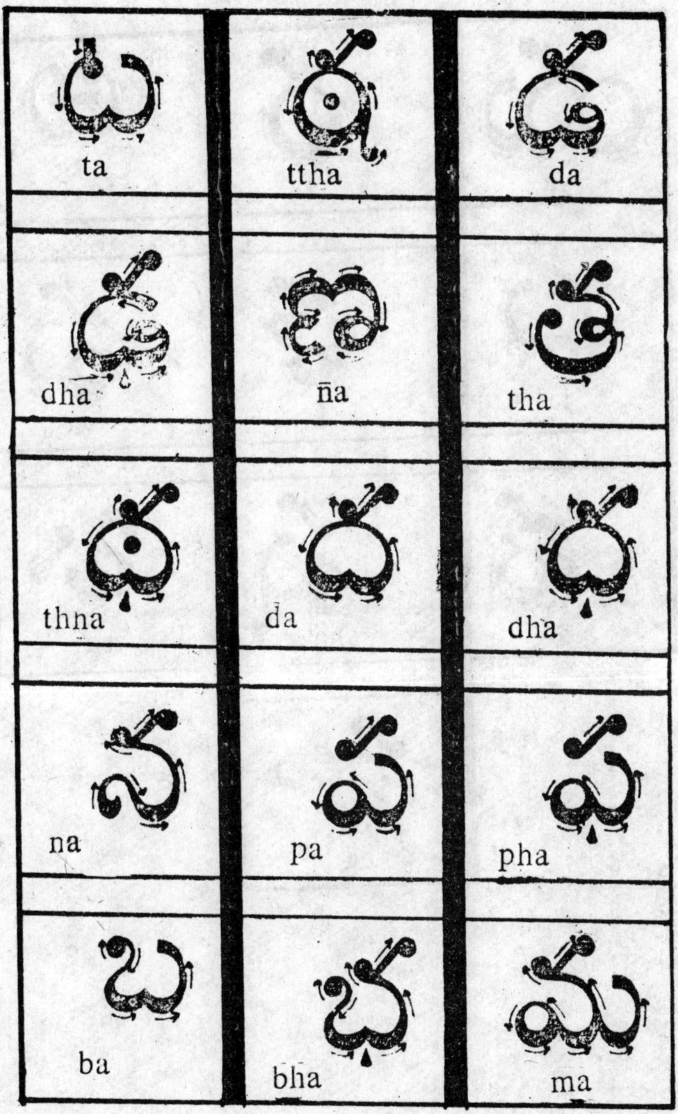
ta
ttha
da
dha
ña
tha
thna
da
dha
na
pa
pha
ba
bha
ma

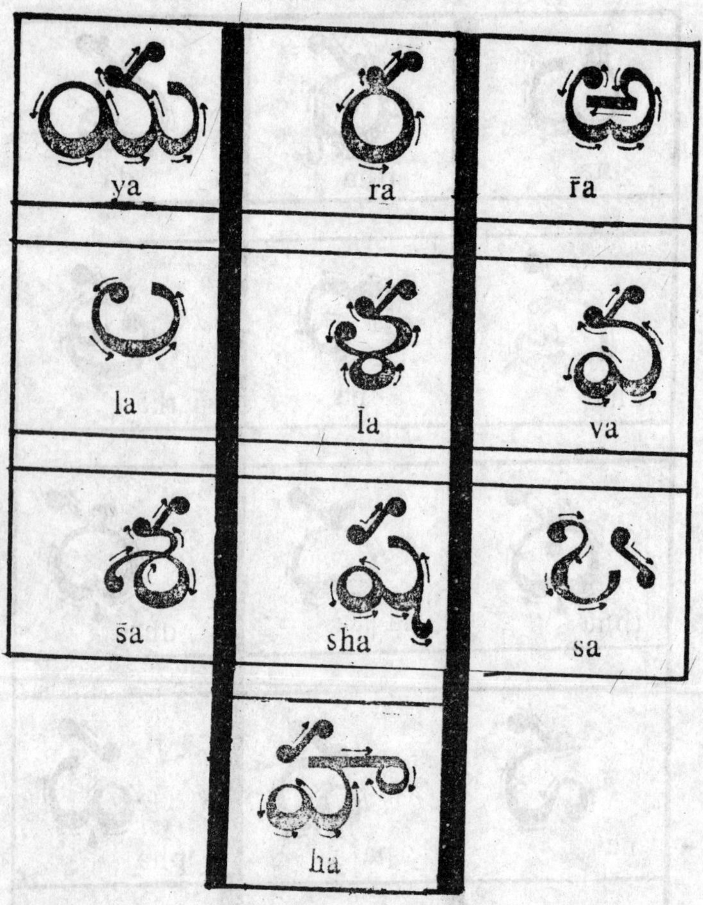
ya
ra
r̄a
la
l̄a
va
s̄a
sha
sa
ha

letters to denote particular Telugu sounds throughout this book and such English letters are given in column 5 against the respective Telugu Alphabet).

Vowels CHART 2

Full form	Short form	Pro-nunciation	As in the word	In this book given as	Nature of the sound of the letters
1	2	3	4	5	6
అ	✓	u	*u*p		short
ఆ	ా	o	*o*n	(aa) a	long
ఇ	ి	i	*i*t	i	short
ఈ	ీ	ee	k*ee*p	ee	long.
ఉ	ు	u	p*u*t	u	short
ఊ	ూ	oo	p*oo*r	oo	long
ఋ	ృ	ri	K*ri*shna	ri	short
ౠ	ౄ	roo	*	*	long
ఌ	ౢ	li	*	*	short
ౡ	ౣ	loo	*	*	long
ఎ	ె	e	p*e*n	e	short
ఏ	ే	a	f*a*ce	ē	long
ఐ	ై	i	f*i*re	ī	long
ఒ	ొ	o	d*o*nation	o	short
ఓ	ో	o	m*o*re	O	long
ఔ	ౌ	ou	*ou*t	ou	long
ఁ	ఁ	*	*	*	*
ం	ం	m, n	su*m*, i*n*k	m, n	short
ః	ః	h	Re*h*man	h	short

* This is a *silent* sign called arasunna. It may be learnt in the later stages.

Consonants CHART 3

Full form	Short form	Pronunciation	As in the word	In this book given as	Nature of the sound of the letters
1	2	3	4	5	6
క	్క	k	ta*k*e	k	
ఖ	్ఖ	kh	(*k*han)	kh	
గ	్గ	g	big	g	
ఘ	్ఘ	gh	*gh*ost	gh	
ఙ	్ఙ	n	ta*nk*	*	not used in elementary stages
చ	్చ	ch	mat*ch*	*ch*	
ౘ	్ౘ	ch	,,	ch	slight dental sound
ఛ	్ఛ	chh	*cha*lk	chh	
జ	్జ	j	*j*et	j	
ౙ	్ౙ	j	,,	j	slight dental sound
ఝ	్ఝ	jh	(j*he*lum)	jh	
ఞ	్ఞ	n	bench	*	not used in elementary stages
ట	్ట	t	hut	t	
ఠ	్ఠ	tth	(mu*tth*)	tth	pronounce forcibly
డ	్డ	d	go*d*	d	
ఢ	్ఢ	dh	*	dh	pronounce forcibly
ణ	్ణ	n	*	ñ	a sound similar to but harsher than 'n'
త	్త	th	wi*th*	*th*	
థ	్థ	th	*th*under	thh	
ద	్ద	th	*th*at	*d*	
ధ	్ధ	dh	(Ra*dha*)	*dh*	[as
న	్న	n	gu*n*	n	న is also written

Consonants CHART 3—*(conud.)*

Full form	Short form	Pronunciation	As in the word	In this book given as	Nature of the Sound of the letters
1	2	3	4	5	6
ప	్ప	p	cu*p*	p	
ఫ	్ఫ	p'	sitha*ph*al	ph	a letter different from the sound of 'f'
బ	్బ	b	ni*b*	b	
భ	్భ	bh	a*bh*or	bh	
మ	్మ	m	*m*an	m	
య	్య	y	*y*et	y	
ర	్ర	r	*r*un	r	These two letters are almost similar in-sound.
ఱ	్ఱ	r	,,	r̄	
ల	్ల	l	ca*ll*	l	
ళ	్ళ	l	*	l̄	a sound similar to but harsher than 'l'
వ	్వ	v	love	v	
శ	్శ	s	que*s*tion	s̄	
ష	్ష	sh	*sh*ot	sh	
స	్స	s	*yes*	s	
హ	్హ	h	*h*ow	h	

Now, pronounce the following Telugu words correctly with the help of the fore-going chart :—

*అలమర	alamara	= almirah	అచట	achata	= there
దయగల	d̄ayagala	= kind	ఇచట	ichata	= here
పడమర	paḍamara	= west	పడవ	padava	= boat
మన గడ	managada	= our pole	పలక	palaka	= slate
గణ గణ	gaña gaña	= sonud of a bell	జనత	janatha	= people
గబ గబ	gaba gaba	= quickly	మరక	maraka	= spot
ఆలమంద	aalamand̄a	= cowherd	వరద	varad̄a	= floot
తలగడ	thalagada	= pillow	మడత	madatha	= fold
హర హర	Hara Hara	= O God siva	గడప	gadapa	= doorstill
			బయట	bayata	= out

* These words are given only as a practice for recognising letters, but not as vocabulary. Therefore, the words or their meanings need *not* be got by heart.

Observe the following examples :—

kaaya	కాయ	= fruit	baana	బాన	= big pot
kaada	కాడ	= stalk	baasa	బాస	= vow
gaadha	గాఢ	= deep	baad̄ha	బాధ	= pain
jaava	జావ	= gruel	baala	బాల	= girl
jaaya	జాయ	= wife	baata	బాట	= way
jaaña	జాణ	= a clever woman	maata	మాట	= word
paata	పాట	= song	matha	మాత	= mother
paaka	పాక	= hut	mama	మామ	= father-in-law
paatha	పాత	= old	maaya	మాయ	= magic
baava	బావ	= brother-in-law	raaja	రాజ	= royal

raama	రామ	= a female	vari	వరి	= paddy crop
vaana	వాన	= rain	kari	కరి	= elephant
vaatha	వాత	= brand	nadi	నది	= river
Saala	శాల	= hall	thadi	తడి	= wet
saana	సాన	= grinding stone	adi	అది	= it
giri	గిరి	= hill	neeli	నీలి	= blue
siri	సిరి	= wealth	geetha	గీత	= line
piriki	పిరికి	= timid	cheema	చీమ	= ant
badi	బడి	= school			

Letters to which the ా mark is attached are giving the long sound *aa* ఆ, as,

కా kaa, గా gaa, జా jaa, పా paa, బా baa, etc. Letters with the ి mark are giving the short sound *i* ఇ; as, గి gi, రి ri, సి si, పి pi, కి ki, డి di, ది di, etc.

Letters with the ీ mark are sounding the long *ee* ఈ, as, నీ nee, గీ gee, వీ vee, చీ chee, etc.

These marks ా, ి ీ, etc., are the short forms of the first 19 letters of the Alphabet. These are given in column 2 of chart 2. By adding these short forms to letters beginning with *k*a క in the Alphabet, different sounds are produced.

For example, take ka క.

క + ా = కా kaa	క + ృ = కృ kru	క + ో = కో kō
క + ి = కి ki	క + ె = కె ke	క + ౌ = కౌ kou
క + ీ = కీ kee	క + ే = కే kē	క + ఁ = కఁ ka
క + ు = కు ku	క + ై = కై kī	క + ం = కం kam
క + ూ = కూ koo	క + ొ = కొ ko	క + ః = కః kah

These different sounds may be applied to any letter in the Alphabet beginning with ka క, as given in the following chart 3. Please go through it carefully.

Consonants. Simple formations.

	+అ	+ఆ	+ఇ	+ఈ	+ఉ	+ఊ	+ఋ	+ఎ	+ఏ	+ఐ	+ఒ	+ఓ	+ఔ	+అం
క్	క	కా	కి	కీ	కు	కూ	కృ	కె	కే	కై	కొ	కో	కౌ	కం
k	ka	kā	ki	kee	ku	koo	kri	ke	kē	kī	ko	kō	kou	kam
ఖ్	ఖ	ఖా	ఖి	ఖీ	ఖు	ఖూ	—	ఖె	ఖే	ఖై	ఖొ	ఖో	ఖౌ	ఖం
kh	kha	khā	khi	khee	khu	khoo	—	khe	khē	khī	kho	khō	khou	kham
గ్	గ	గా	గి	గీ	గు	గూ	గృ	గె	గే	గై	గొ	గో	గౌ	గం
g	ga	gā	gi	gee	gu	goo	gri	ge	gē	gī	go	gō	gou	gam
ఘ్	ఘ	ఘా	ఘి	ఘీ	ఘు	ఘూ	ఘృ	ఘె	ఘే	ఘై	ఘొ	ఘో	ఘౌ	ఘం
gh	gha	ghā	ghi	ghee	ghu	ghoo	ghri	ghe	ghē	ghī	gho	ghō	ghou	gham
చ్	చ	చా	చి	చీ	చు	చూ	చృ	చె	చే	చై	చొ	చో	చౌ	చం
ch	cha	chā	chi	chee	chu	choo	—	che	chē	chī	cho	chō	chou	cham
జ్	జ	జా	జి	జీ	జు	జూ	—	జె	జే	జై	జొ	జో	జౌ	జం
j	ja	jā	ji	jee	ju	joo	—	je	jē	jī	jo	jō	jou	jam
ట్	ట	టా	టి	టీ	టు	టూ	—	టె	టే	టై	టొ	టో	టౌ	టం
t	ta	tā	ti	tee	tu	too	—	te	tē	tī	to	tō	tou	tam
డ్	డ	డా	డి	డీ	డు	డూ	—	డె	డే	డై	డొ	డో	డౌ	డం
d	da	dā	di	dee	du	doo	—	de	dē	dī	do	dō	dou	dam
ణ్	ణ	ణా	ణి	ణీ	ణు	ణూ	—	ణె	ణే	ణై	ణొ	ణో	ణౌ	ణం
ñ	ña	ñā	ñi	ñee	ñu	ñoo	—	ñe	ñē	ñī	ño	ñō	ñou	ñam

	+ అ	+ ఆ	+ ఇ	+ ఈ	+ ఉ	+ ఊ	+ ఋ	+ ఎ	+ ఏ	+ ఐ	+ ఒ	+ ఓ	+ ఔ	+ ం
త్	త	తా	తి	తీ	తు	తూ	తృ	తె	తే	తై	తొ	తో	తౌ	తం
th	tha	thā	thi	thee	thu	thoo	thri	the	thē	thī	tho	thō	thou	tham
ద్	ద	దా	ది	దీ	దు	దూ	దృ	దె	దే	దై	దొ	దో	దౌ	దం
d̄	d̄a	d̄ā	d̄i	dee	d̄u	d̄oo	d̄ri	d̄e	d̄ē	d̄ī	d̄o	d̄ō	d̄ou	d̄am
న్	న	నా	ని	నీ	ను	నూ	నృ	నె	నే	నై	నొ	నో	నౌ	నం
n	na	nā	ni	nee	nu	noo	nri	ne	nē	nī	no	nō	nou	nam
ప్	ప	పా	పి	పీ	పు	పూ	పృ	పె	పే	పై	పొ	పో	పౌ	పం
p	pa	pā	pi	pee	pu	poo	pri	pe	pē	pī	po	pō	pou	pam
బ్	బ	బా	బి	బీ	బు	బూ	బృ	బె	బే	బై	బొ	బో	బౌ	బం
b	ba	bā	bi	bee	bu	boo	bri	be	bē	bī	bo	bō	bou	bam
మ్	మ	మా	మి	మీ	ము	మూ	మృ	మె	మే	మై	మొ	మో	మౌ	మం
m	ma	mā	mi	mee	mu	moo	mri	me	mē	mī	mo	mō	mou	mam
య్	య	యా	యి	యీ	యు	యూ	—	యె	యే	యై	యొ	యో	యౌ	యం
y	ya	yā	yi	yee	yu	yoo	—	ye	yē	yī	yo	yō	you	yam
ర్	ర	రా	రి	రీ	రు	రూ	—	రె	రే	రై	రొ	రో	రౌ	రం
r	ra	rā	ri	ree	ru	roo	—	re	rē	rī	ro	rō	rou	ram
ఱ్	ఱ	ఱా	ఱి	ఱీ	ఱు	ఱూ	—	ఱె	ఱే	ఱై	ఱొ	ఱో	ఱౌ	ఱం
r̄	r̄a	r̄ā	r̄i	r̄ee	r̄u	r̄oo	—	r̄e	r̄ē	r̄ī	r̄o	r̄ō	r̄ou	r̄am

Consonants—(Contd.)

	+ అ	+ ఆ	+ ఇ	+ ఈ	+ ఉ	+ ఊ	+ ఋ	+ ఎ	+ ఏ	+ ఐ	+ ఒ	+ ఓ	+ ఔ	+ ం
ల్	ల	లా	లి	లీ	లు	లూ	—	లె	లే	లై	లొ	లో	లౌ	లం
l	la	lā	li	lee	lu	loo	—	le	lē	lī	lo	lō	lou	lam
ళ్	ళ	ళా	ళి	ళీ	ళు	ళూ	—	ళె	ళే	ళై	ళొ	ళో	ళౌ	ళం
l̄	l̄a	l̄ā	l̄i	l̄ee	l̄u	l̄oo	—	l̄e	l̄ē	l̄ī	l̄o	l̄ō	l̄ou	l̄am
వ్	వ	వా	వి	వీ	వు	వూ	—	వె	వే	వై	వొ	వో	వౌ	వం
v	va	vā	vi	vee	vu	voo	vri	ve	vē	vī	vo	vō	vou	vam
శ్	శ	శా	శి	శీ	శు	శూ	శృ	శె	శే	శై	శొ	శో	శౌ	శం
s̄	s̄a	s̄ā	s̄i	s̄ee	s̄u	s̄oo	s̄ri	s̄e	s̄ē	s̄ī	s̄o	s̄ō	s̄ou	s̄am
ష్	ష	షా	షి	షీ	షు	షూ	షృ	షె	షే	షై	షొ	షో	షౌ	షం
sh	sha	shā	shi	shee	shu	shoo	—	she	shē	shī	sho	shō	shou	sham
స్	స	సా	సి	సీ	సు	సూ	సృ	సె	సే	సై	సొ	సో	సౌ	సం
s	sa	sā	si	see	su	soo	—	se	sē	sī	so	sō	sou	sam
హ్	హ	హా	హి	హీ	హు	హూ	—	హె	హే	హై	హొ	హో	హౌ	హం
h	ha	hā	hi	hee	hu	hoo	hri	he	hē	hī	ho	hō	hou	ham

Now, read the following words with the help of chart No. 3 :—

కుడి	kudi	= right	సూది	soo-d̄i	= needle
గుడి	gu-di	= temple	గెల	gela	= bunch
తుది	thu-d̄i	= last	చెడు	che-du	= bad
ధుని	d̄huni	= flow	తెలివి	the-li-vi	= cleverness
నుసి	nusi	= wood power	నెపము	ne-pa-mu	= excuse
పులి	puli	= tiger	పెనము	pe-na-mu	= pan
ముడి	mudi	= raw	మెడ	me-da	= neck
శుచి	Šuchĭ	= clean-liness	రెండు	ren-du	= two
			వెంట	ven-ta	= along with
సుధ	sud̄ha	= nectar			
ఊరు	oo-ru	= village	సెగ	se-ga	= heat
కూర	koo-ra	= curry	గేదె	gē-de	= buffalo
గూని	goo-ni	= hunch-back	చేటు	chētu	= harm
ఘూకము	ghoo-ka-mu	= owl	డేగ	dē-ga	= hawk
చూర	choo-ra	= powder	తేనె	thēne	= honey
జూలు	joo-lu	= mane	తేలు	thē-lu	= scorpion
తూము	thoo-mu	= sluice	దేవుడు	de-vu-du	= God
తూరుపు	thoo.ru-pu	= east	నేత	ne-tha	= weaving
తూనిక	thoo-ni-ka	= weight	పేరు	pē-ru	= name
నూలు	noo-lu	= yarn	మేడ	mē-da	= up-stairs
నూయి	noo-yi	= well	మేక	mē-ka	= goat
పూవు	poo-vu	= flower	రేఖ	rēkha	= line
బూజు	boo-ju	= cob	లేడి	lē-di	= stag
		wed	వేడి	vē-di	= hot
మూత	moo-tha	= cover	వేరు	vē-ru	= root
రూక	roo-ka	= rupee	కైత	kī-tha	= poetry
శూరుడు	Šoo-ru.du	= brave	ఖైదు	khīdu	= jail
		man	పైరు	pī-ru	= crop

మైనము	mi-na-mu	= wax	సోది	sō-di	= long talk
కొడుకు	ko-du-ku	= son			
గొడుగు	go-du-gu	= umbrella	గౌను	gou-nu	= gown
దొర	d̄o-ra	= gentleman	చౌక	chouka	= cheap
పొడి	po-di	= powder	తౌడు	thou-du	= bran
కోడలు	kō-da-lu	= daughter-in-law	దౌడ	d̄ouda	= jaw
			నౌక	nou-ka	= ship
కోడి	kōdi	= cock	పౌను	pou-nu	= pound (lb)
గోడ	gō-da	= wall			
చోటు	chō-tu	= place	మౌనము	mou-na-mu	= silence
డోలు	dōlu	= drum	రౌతు	rou-thu	= a horse-man
తోక	thōka	= tail			
తోట	thōta	= garden	కంఠము	kan-ttha-mu	= neck
దోర	d̄ō-ra	= half-ripe	గంట	ganta	= bell
నోరు	nōru	= mouth	జంట	jan-ta	= pair
పోరు	pō-ru	= struggle	పందెము	pan-de-mu	= race
మోత	mōtha	= carrying	కాంతి	kaanthi	= light
రోజు	rōju	= day	పిండి	pin-di	= flour
లోటు	lō-tu	= defect	దొంగ	d̄onga	= thief
శోకము	sō-ka-mu	= sorrow	రంగు	rangu	= colour
శోష	sō-sha	= weakness	కొంత	kontha	= some

మంచి manchi = good

Read the following words with the help of the English spelling given against each of them :—

a-kka	అక్క	= elder sister	na-kka	నక్క	= fox
cha-kka	చెక్క	= plank	cha-kka-ni	చక్కని	= beautiful
le-kka	లెక్క	= account	bu-gga	బుగ్గ	= cheek
o-kka	ఒక్క	= one	tha-gga	తగ్గ	= fit
va-kka	వక్క	= betel-nut	ma-gga-mu	మగ్గము	= loom

Note that the double sound of *kka* is got by adding the sign ్క below the letter క, as క్క, and the double sound of *gga* is got by adding the sign ్గ below the letter

గ as గ్గ. You will observe that these signs ్క & ్గ are the short forms of the letters క ka and గ ga as shown in column 2 of Chart 3.

Now try to read the following words with double sounds with the help of the English spelling given against each word :—

anna	అన్న	= brother	go-ppa	గొప్ప	= great
annamu	అన్నము	= food	C̄ho-ppa	చొప్ప	= hay
kannamu	కన్నము	= hole	a-bba	అబ్బ	= oh!
dunna	దున్న	= he-buffalo	bo-bha	బొబ్బ	= blister
			a-yya	అయ్య	= father
amma	అమ్మ	= mother	ko-yya	కొయ్య	= wood
kummari	కుమ్మరి	= potter	S̄a-yya	శయ్య	= bed
komma	కొమ్మ	= branch	e-r̄r̄a-ṇi	ఎఱ్ఱని	= red
echchata	ఎచ్చట	= where	ka-r̄r̄a	కఱ్ఱ	= stick
bichchamu	బిచ్చము	= alms	pa-r̄r̄a	పఱ్ఱ	= waste land
vechchana	వెచ్చన	= heat			
bo-jja	బొజ్జ	= stomach	e-lla	ఎల్ల	= boundary
o-jja	ఒజ్జ	= teacher	ka-lla	కల్ల	= false
ka-tta	కట్ట	= bundle	cha-lla	చల్ల	= butter-milk
batta	బట్ట	= cloth			
tha-tta	తట్ట	= basket	ba-lla	బల్ల	= table or bench
bidda	బిడ్డ	= child			
gadda	గడ్డ	= boil	bi-l̄l̄a	బిళ్ళ	= disc
a-ththa	అత్త	= mother-in-law	a-vva	అవ్వ	= (old) lady
			bu-vva	బువ్వ	= food
na-ththa	నత్త	= snail	ga-vva	గవ్వ	= shell
me-ththa	మెత్త	= pillow	mukku	ముక్కు	= nose
ped̄d̄a	పెద్ద	= big	bo-ggu	బొగ్గు	= charcoal
mu-d̄d̄a	ముద్ద	= a mouth-full	ga-chchu	గచ్చు	= cement
			ga-jji	గజ్జి	= itch
ka-ppa	కప్ప	= frog	ka-ttu	కట్టు	= bandage

va-ddi	వడ్డి—interest	sa-bbu	సబ్బు—soap
ka-ththi	కత్తి—sword	so-mmu	సొమ్ము—jewellery
pa-d̄d̄u	పద్దు—item	ba-r̄r̄e	బఱ్ఱె—she-baffalo
ka-nnu	కన్ను—eye	tha-lli	తల్లి—mother
a-ppu	అప్పు—debt		

Now, see from chart No. 2, which short forms are similar in shape to their original letters and which are completely different from them. You will observe that the following short forms are quite different from their original letters :—

The short forms of the first 8 letters (consonants).

క	ka	్క	య	ya	్య
త	tha	్త	ర	ra	్ర
న	na	్న	ల	la	్ల
మ	ma	్మ	వ	va	్వ

The short forms of all other letters are very much like the original letters. Therefore, it is very easy to remember them.

e.g. గ—్గ జ—్జ ప—్ప
చ—్చ ద—్ద బ—్బ

Remove the top stroke ✓ and you will get the short forms.

Now read the following words with the help of the English spelling given against them :—

aaryudu	ఆర్యుడు	=	an Aryan
ul-ka	ఉల్క	=	meteor
naal-gu	నాల్గు	=	four
Ōr-pu	ఓర్పు	=	patience
bhaar-ya	భార్య	=	wife
soor-yu-du	సూర్యుడు	=	sun

chan-d̄ru-du చంద్రుడు = moon
na-ksha-thra-mu నక్షత్రము = star
cha-kra-mu చక్రము = wheel

Difficult letters as those shown above are given in the following chart No. 4, which may be referred to whenever the student is in doubt about the pronunciation of a difficult letter.

Important double and compound letter formations (called conjunct consonants) are given below. These are shown here with the first vowel అ *(a)* added on to them and they can be altered to add any other vowel as already shown in the previous pages.

క్క	k-ka	ఖ్య	k-h-ya	జ్ర	j-ra	త్క	th-ka
క్చ	k-cha	గ్గ	g-ga	జ్వ	j-va	త్న	th-na
క్ట	k-ta	గ్ద	g-da	ట్ట	t-ṭa	త్ప	th-pa
క్థ	k-tha	గ్ధ	g-d̄ha	ట్క	t-ka	త్ఫ	th-pha
క్త్ర	k-th-ra	గ్న	g-na	ట్న	t-na	త్మ	th-ma
క్త్వ	k-th-va	గ్మ	g-ma	ట్ప	t-pa	త్య	th-ya
క్న	k-na	గ్య	g-ya	ట్మ	t-ma	త్ర	th-ra
క్ప	k-pa	గ్ర	g-ra	ట్య	t-ya	త్ర్య	th-r-ya
క్ప్ర	k-p-ra	గ్ర్య	g-r-ya	ట్ర	t-ra	త్ల	th-la
క్బ	k-ba	గ్ల	g-la	ట్ల	t-la	త్వ	th-va
క్మ	k-ma	గ్వ	g-va	ట్వ	t-va	త్త్వ	th th-va
క్య	k-ya	ఘ్న	gh-na	ట్స	t-sa	త్స	th-sa
క్ర	k-ra	ఘ్ర	gh-ra	థ్య	tth-ya	త్స్య	th-s-ya
క్ర్య	k-r-ya	చ్చ	ch-cha	డ్గ	d-ga	థ్య	thh-ya
క్ల	k-la	చ్ఛ	ch-chha	డ్డ	d-da	ద్గ	d̄-ga
క్వ	k-va	చ్ఛ్ర	ch-chh-ra	డ్య	d-ya	ద్ధ	d̄-d̄ha
క్ష	k-sha	చ్ఛ్వ	ch-chh-va	ద్ర	d̄-ra	ద్ఘ	d̄-gha
		చ్య	ch-ya	డ్ల	d-la	ద్భ	d̄-bha

క్ష్ణ	k-sh-ña	జ్ఞ	j-na	డ్వ	d-va	ద్భ్య	d̄-bh-ya
క్ష్మ	k-sh-ma	జ్జ	j-ja	ధ్ర	dh-ra	ద్మ	d̄-ma
క్ష్య	k-sh-ya	జ్మ	j-ma	ధ్య	dh-ya	ద్న	d̄-na
క్స	k-sa	జ్య	j-ya	ఙ్క	ñ-nk	ద్ర	d́-ra
ద్ర్య	d̄-r-ya	బ్ధ	b-d̄ha	ర్న	r-na	వ్ర	v-ra
ద్వ	d̄-va	బ్బ	b-ba	ర్ప	r-pa	వ్వ	v-va
ద్వ్య	d̄-v-ya	బ్య	b-ya	ర్బ	r-ba	శ్చ	s-cha
ధ్న	d̄h-na	బ్ర	b-ra	ర్భ	r-bha	శ్న	s̄-na
ధ్మ	d̄h-ma	బ్ల	b-la	ర్మ	r-ma	శ్మ	s̄-ma
ధ్య	d̄h-ya	బ్వ	b-va	ర్మ్య	r-m-ya	శ్య	s-ya
ధ్ర	d̄h-ra	భ్య	bh-ya	ర్య	r-ya	శ్ర	s̄-ra
ధ్వ	d̄h-va	భ్ర	bh-ra	ర్ల	r-la	శ్ల	s̄-la
న్క	n-ka	భ్వ	bh-va	ర్వ	r va	శ్వ	s̄-va
న్గ	n-ga	మ్న	m-na	ర్శ	r-s̄a	శ్శ	s̄-s̄a
న్త	n-tha	మ్మ	m-m-	ర్శ్య	r-s̄-ya	ష్క	sh-ka
న్న	n-na	మ్య	m-ya	ర్ష	r-sha	ష్క్ర	sh-k-ra
న్మ	n-ma	మ్ర	m-ra	ర్హ	r-ha	ష్ట	sh-ta
న్య	n-ya	మ్ల	m-la	ఱ్ఱ	r̄-r̄a	ష్ట్య	sh-tya
న్ర	n-ra	య్డ	y-da	ల్క	l-ka	ష్ట్ర	sh-t-ra
న్వ	n-va	య్వ	y-va	ల్గ	l-ga	ష్ణ	sh-ña
న్ష	n-sha	ర్క	r-ka	ల్ట	l-ta	ష్ప	sh-pa
న్స	n-sa	ర్గ	rga	ల్డ	l-da	ష్ప్ర	sh-p-ra
ప్డ	p-da	ర్ఘ	r-gha	ల్త	l-thᵣa	ష్మ	sh-ma
ప్త	p-tha	ర్చ	r-cha	ల్ద	l-d̄a	ష్య	sh-ya
ప్న	p-na	ర్జ	r-ja	ల్న	l-na	ష్వ	sh-va
ప్ప	p-pa	ర్డ	r-da	ల్ప	l-pa	స్క	s-ka
ప్మ	p-ma	ర్ణ	r-na	ల్మ	l-ma	స్త	s-tha
ప్య	p-ya	ర్ణ్య	r-ñ-ya	ల్య	l-ya	స్ప	s-pa
ప్ర	p-ra	ర్త	r-tha	ల్ల	l-la	స్మ	s-ma

ప్ల	p-la	ర్థ	r-tha	ల్వ	l-va	స్య	s-ya
ప్స	p-sa	ర్ద	r-ḏa	ల్హ	l-ha	స్ర	s-ra
బ్జ	b-ja	ర్ధ	r-ḏha	ళ్ళ	ḻ-ḻa	స్ల	s-la
బ్ద	b-da	ర్ధ్వ	r-ḏh-v-a	వ్య	v-ya	స్వ	s-va
స్స	s-sa	హ్న	h-na	హ్య	h-ya	హ్ల	h-la
హ్ఞ	h-ña	హ్మ	h-ma	హ్ర	h-ra	హ్వ	h-va

A few examples of forming conjunct consonants (double or compound letters) with the other vowels are given below :—

క్కి	k-ki	త్ర్యం	th-r-yam
క్మి	k-mi	ప్డు	p-du
క్రూ	k-roo	ప్లె	p-le
గ్రే	g-re	ర్చీ	r-chee
గ్గీ	g-gī	బ్రౌ	b-rou
జ్వా	j-vā	చ్చి	ch-chi
డ్డా	d-dā		

From the above examples, it will be seen that, in Telugu, the first letter of a conjunct consonant is written in its full form and the remaining letters are added on to it in their short forms.

The short forms of letters have their own vernacular names which are given below for the information of the student.

full form	short form	Vernacular name	pronunciation
అ	✓	తలకట్టు	thalakattu
ఆ	ా	దీర్ఘము	ḏeerghamu
ఇ	ి	గుడి	gudi
ఈ	ీ	గుడిదీర్ఘము	gudi deer
ఉ	ు	కొమ్ము	kommu

full form	short form	Vernacular name	pronunciation
ఊ	ూ	కొమ్ముదీర్ఘము	kommu deerghamu
ఋ	ృ	వట్రుసుడి	vatrusudi
ౠ	ౄ	వట్రుసుడిదీర్ఘము	vatrusudideerghamu
ఎ	ె	ఎత్వము	ethvamu
ఏ	ే	ఏత్వము	ēthvamu
ఐ	ై	ఐత్వము	Īthvamu
ఒ	ొ	ఒత్వము	othvamu
ఓ	ో	ఓత్వము	Ōthvamu
ఔ	ౌ	ఔత్వము	outhvamu
ం	ం	సున్న	sunna (zero)
ః	ః	విసర్గము	visargamu
క	్క	కావత్తు	kā vaththu
ఖ	్ఖ	ఖావత్తు	khā vaththu
...	...	...	...
మ	్మ	మావత్తు	mā vaththu
య	్య	క్యావడి	kyā vadi
ర	్ర	క్రావడి, రేఫ	krā vadi, or repha
ల	్ల	లావత్తు	lā vathu
...	...	...	...
హ	్హ	హావత్తు	ha vaththu.

(*N. B.* :– The names of the short forms of the letters omitted above may be known by adding the term వత్తు (vath-thu) to each such letter.

e. g. గ — ్గ గావత్తు gā-vaththu

వ — ్వ వావత్తు vā-vaththu,

The difference in pronunciation of the letters of the following sets cannot be explained here and it is, therefore better to try to know them personally.

చ, చే; జ జే; ఢ, ధ; న, ణ;

ఋ, ర, ఱ; ఌ, ల, ళ, ళ. స; ః, హా.

Visarga (ః) does not generally occur in Telugu Vocabulary of a routine nature, except in the word దుఃఖము (ḏuhkhamu) meaning "sorrow." The letters ఙ and ఞ also do not occur frequently, with the exception of the word జ్ఞానము (Gnanamu), meaning "knowledge."

In Telugu, there is a sign called అరసున్న (arasunna) or semi-circle which once used to represent a nasal or seminasal sound. But of late, it does not appear to possess any special sound and is used only to differentiate similar words having different meanings.

LESSON 2

Prepositions

ki కి, ku కు—to
kī కై· kor̄aku కోఅకు
kōsamu కోసము ku కు } —for
goorchi గూర్చి
gur̄inchi గుంచిని } —about
lō లో, lōpala లోవల—in, among
chē చే, chētha చేత—by
thō తో·. thōda తోడ—with
nundi నుండి—from
valana వలన, valla వల్ల—by
kante కంటె—than
yodḍa యొద్ద—at (with)
dvārā ద్వారా—through
pī పై· pīni పైని, meeda మీద—on, upon
pīki పైకి—up
var̄aku వఱకు—upto
lōniki లోనికి—into
mundu ముందు—before
venuka వెనుక—behind
venta వెంట—along with

vīpu వైపు—towards
yokka యొక్క—of
chuttu చుట్టు—around
krinda క్రింద—under, underneath
prakka ప్రక్క—beside (by the side of)
bayata బయట—out, outside
anthata అంతట—by oneself everywhere ?
dooramu దూరము—distance, far
paḍi పది—ten
pillavādu పిల్లవాడు—boy
dabbu డబ్బు—money
āta ఆట—play, show, game
thōlu తోలు—to drive
thrāgu త్రాగు—to drink
mā మా—our. mee —your
idigō ఇదిగో—this,
ivigō ఇవిగో—these

A Objective case (*ni* ని & *nu* ను)

Read the following sentences :—

1. Rāmudu Krishnuni PiluČhuchunnāḍu
   రాముడు కృష్ణుని పిలుచుచున్నాడు—**Rāma is calling Krishna.**
2. Rāmudu kukkanu kottuČhunnāḍu
   రాముడు కుక్కను కొట్టుచున్నాడు—**Rāma is beating (the) dog.**
3. Rāmudu āvunu ČhooČhuČhunnāḍu
   రాముడు ఆవును చూచుచున్నాడు—**Rāma is seeing (a) cow.**

In the above three sentences, the word Rāmuḍu రాముడు denotes the subject, the doer of the action, and each of the words Krishnuni కృష్ణుని Kukkanu కుక్కను, āvunu ఆవును denote the object, the sufferer (or the experiences) of the action. Words which are objects in a sentence are said to be in the *objective case.*

In English, words in the objective case are known from their meanings and from the relative position occupied by them in the sentence. But in Telugu, *ni* ని, or *nu* ను is added to the word in the objective case. If such a word denotes a lifeless beings, this *ni* ని, or *nu* ను is usually omitted.

e. g. Rāmudu Pandlu thinuČhunnāḍu
రాముడు పండ్లు తినుచున్నాడు—Rāma is eating fruits.

Krishnudu annamu thinuČhunnāḍu
కృష్ణుడు అన్నము తినుచున్నాడు—Krishna is eating food.

In the above two sentences the objects fruit and food lifeless things. Therefore, ని *ni* or ను *nu* is not added to the words పండ్లు Pandlu and అన్నము annamu.

Now let us know when ని *ni* is used and when ను *nu* is used. * Observe the following words :—

	Words	*Objective case*
(a)	Rāmu*du* రాముడు	—Rāmuni రాముని
	Krishnu*du* కృష్ణుడు	—Krishnuni కృష్ణుని
	bālu*du* బాలుడు	—bāluni బాలుని (boy)
	manushyu*du* మనుష్యుడు	— manushyuni మనుష్యుని (man)
	sēvaku*du* సేవకుడు	—sēvakuni సేవకుని

* * * *

(b) hari హరి – harini హరిని
Lakshmi లక్ష్మి—Lakshmini లక్ష్మిని
yajamāni యజమాని—yajamānini యజమానిని
pilli పిల్లి—pillini పిల్లిని
kāki కాకి—kākini కాకిని
kurch*ee* కుర్చీ—kurcheeni కుర్చీని

* * * *

(c) kukk*a* కుక్క—kukkanu కుక్కను
amm*a* అమ్మ – ammanu అమ్మను (mother)
pitt*a* పిట్ట—pittanu పిట్టను (bird)

---

* Application of these prepositional (case) terminations to nouns in the plural number is dealt with later on in the lesson.

anna అన్న—annanu అన్నను (brother)
ayya అయ్య—ayyanu అయ్యను (father)

*　　*　　*

(d) guṟṟamu గుఱ్ఱము—guṟṟamunu గుఱ్ఱమును
āvu ఆవు—āvunu ఆవును
eddu ఎద్దు—eddunu ఎద్దును
gēde గేదె—gēdenu గేదెను

From the above examples, we find that *ni* ని is added (to form the objective case) to :

(a) personal nouns * ending in *du* డు, after removing that *du* డు: and to

(b) all nouns ending in ī ఇ

We find also that *nu* ను is added (to form the objective case) to nouns other than those mentioned in (a) and (b) above. In other words, *nu* ను is added to nouns ending in.

(c) *a* ు, ā ా, *e* ె, and
(d) *u* ు but not *du* డు.

The above rules apply to nouns denoting living beings only. The student is reminded that no change is necessary on the objective case forms of nouns denoting lifeless things.

B. To (*ki* కి *ku* కు or *naku* నకు)

Read the following words :—

(a) anna*ku* అన్నకు—to (the) brother
amma*ku* అమ్మకు—to (the) mother

---

* Application of prepositional (case) terminations to PRONOUNS is dealt with later on in another lesson.

ayy*aku* అయ్యకు—to (the) father
b$^{\bar{a}}$t*aku* బాటకు—to (the) way
jendā*ku* జెండాకు—to (the) flag
gamp*aku* గంపకు—to (the) basket
kukk*aku* కుక్కకు—to (the) dog

(b) gē$\bar{d}$*eku* గేదెకు—to (the) buffalo
bar̄r̄*eku* బఱ్ఱెకు— ,, ,,
pett*eku* పెట్టెకు—to (the) box.

* * *

(c) āvun*aku* ఆవునకు—to (the) cow
chett*unaku* చెట్టునకు—to (the) tree
gur̄r̄am*unaku* గుఱ్ఱమునకు—to (the) horse
pusthakam*unaku* పుస్తకమునకు—to (the) book
kalam*unaku* కలమునకు—to (the) pen
guruv*unaku* గురువునకు—to (the) teacher

* * *

Also written as

(d) R$^{\bar{a}}$m*unaku* రామునకు—to Rāma (R$^{\bar{a}}$muniki రామునికి)
Krishn*unaku* కృష్ణునకు—to Krishna (Krishnuniki కృష్ణునికి)
bal*unaku* బాలునకు—to (the) boy (baluniki బాలునికి)
manushy*unaku* మనుష్యునకు—to (the) man (manushyuniki మనుష్యునికి)
sēvak*unaku* సేవకునకు—to (the) servant (sēvakuniki సేవకునికి)

(e) thall*iki* తల్లికి—to the mother

thandr*iki* తండ్రికి—to (the) father

pill*iki* పిల్లికి—to (the) cat

kā*ḷiki* కాకికి—to (the) crow

bad*iki* బడికి—to (the) school

yajamāniki యజమానికి—{ to (the) master / to (the) officer }

kurcheek*i* కుర్చీకి—to (the) chair

kachēr*eeki* కచేరీకి—to (the) office

From the above examples we find that in

(a) & (b) k*u* కు is added to nouns ending in *a* (✓) or ē (ా);

(b) *naku* నకు is added to nouns ending in *u* (ు) and *ūdu* ఉడు; and that

(c) k*i* కి is added to nouns ending in (ి), or ee (ీ)

There are some exceptions to these rules. See the following examples :—

(a) kannu కన్ను : kantiki కంటికి—to (the) eye.

mannu మన్ను : mantiki మంటికి—to (the) earth

illu ఇల్లు : intiki ఇంటికి—to (the) house

pallu పల్లు : pantiki పంటికి—to (the) tooth

* * *

(b) thrādu త్రాడు : thrātiki త్రాటికి—to (the) rope.

nōru నోరు : nōtiki నోటికి—to (the) mouth.

nāgali నాగలి : nāgatiki నాగటికి—to (the) plough

(c) chēyi చేయి : chēthiki చేతికి—to (the) hand
gōyi గోయి : gōthiki గోతికి—to (the) pit
nooyi నూయి : noothiki నూతికి—to (the) well
r̄āyi ఱాయి : r̄athiki ఱాతికి—to (the) stone

* * * *

(d) kālu కాలు : kāliki కాలికి—to (the) leg
ooru ఊరు : ooriki ఊరికి—to (the) village

In the above examples, the last letters of the nouns are replaced by *nti* ంటి *ti* టి and *thi* తి in groups (a), (b) and (c) respectively and joined by *i* ఇ in group (d). **Such nouns are to be learnt by observation only.**

All prepositions are added to the altered forms of these words.

C. Other Prepositions :—

All other prepositions (case terminations) given at **the beginning** of the lesson can be applied to nouns as shown below :—

(1) By adding them to the objective case form of personal nouns ending in **du**; as

Rāmunichē	రామునిచే	—by Rāma	
,, thō	తో	—with	,,
,, ki	కై	—for	,,
,, pī	పై	—on	,,
,, gur̄inchi	గురించి	about	,,
,, lō	లో	—in	,,

Rāmuni kante	రాముని కంటె	—than Rāma
,, nundi	,, నుండి	—from ,,
,, valana	,, వలన	—due to ,,
bāluni mundu	బాలుని ముందు	—before the boy
,, vīpu	,, వైపు	—towards ,,
,, pīki	,, పైకి	—on to ,,
,, yokka	,, యొక్క	—of ,,
,, prakka	,, ప్రక్క	—bisides ,,
,, venuka	,, వెనుక	—behind ,,
,, tharuvātha	,, తరువాత	—after ,,
,, Chuttù	,, చుట్టు	—around ,,
,, dvārā	,, ద్వారా	—through ,,

Try similar formations with other nouns such as Krishnuni కృష్ణుని manushyuni మనుష్యుని, sēvakuni సేవకుని, etc., etc.

(2) By adding them (the prepositions) direct to all nouns other than personal nouns ending in **du** డు. *In nouns having altered forms, add the terminations to the altered forms.*

Kaḷāmu thō	కలము తో	—with (the) pen
,, lō	,, లో	—in ,,
,, pī	,, పై	—on ,,
balla chuttu	బల్ల చుట్టు	—around (the) table
,, meeda	,, మీద	—on ,,
,, krinda	,, క్రింద	—under ,,
,, vīpu	,, వైపు	—towards ,,

gampa lō	గంప లో—in (the) basket	
,, meeda	,, మీద—on	,,
gur̄r̄amu pī	గుఱ్ఱము పై—on (the) horse	
,, meeda	,, మీద— ,, ,,	,,
,, venuka	,, వెనక—behind	,,
,, prakka	,, ప్రక్క—beside	,,
kāki yokka	కాకి యొక్క—of (the) crow	
,, kante	,, కంటె—than	,,
,, venta	,, వెంట—along with crow	
yajamāni kor̄aku	యజమాని కొఱకు—for (the) master	
,, nundi	,, నుండి—from	,,
,, d̄vārā	,, ద్వారా—through	,,
,, chētha	,, చేత—by	,,
,, thō	,, తో—with	,,
Inti lō	ఇంటి లో —in (the) house	
,, pī	,, పై —on	,,
,, Chuttu	,, చుట్టు—around	,,
,, venuka	,, వెనుక—behind	,,
kanti meed̄a	కంటి మీద—on (the) eye	
,, lō	,, లో—in	,,
,, thō	,, తో—with	,,
nōti lō	నోటి లో—in (the) mouth	
,, thō	,, తో—with	,,
chēthi lō	చేతి లో—in (the) hand	
,, thō	,, తో—with	,,
,, pī	,, పై—on	,,

rāthi thō రాతి తో—with (the) stone
,, lō ,, లో—in ,,
,, meeda ,, మీద—on ,,
,, krinda ,, క్రింద—under ,,
gōthi lō గోతి లో—in (the) pit ,,
oori lō ఊరి లో—in (the) village
,, vīpu ,, వైపు—towards ,,
,, bayata ,, బయట—outside ,,
,, chuttu ,, చుట్టు—around ,,
kālithō కాలి తో—with (the) leg
,, krinda ,, క్రింద—under ,,
,, meeda ,, మీద—on ,,
amma yokka అమ్మ యొక్క—of (the) mother
,, chētha ,, చేత—by ,,
,, kante ,, కంటె—than ,,
thandri nundi తండ్రి నుండి—from (the) father
,, thō ,, తో—with ,,
,, kante ,, కంటె—than ,,
,, yokka ,, యొక్క—of ,,

In the foregoing examples in (2), we have omitted the termination *goorchi* గూర్చి (*gurinchi* గురించి—about) *This termination is always to be added to the objective case of a noun.*

ammanu goorchi అమ్మను గూర్చి—about (the) mother
gurinchi గురించి

kalamunu goorchi కలమును గూర్చి—about (the) pen
gur̄inchi గురించి

gur̄r̄amunu	,,	గుఱ్ఱమును	,,	—	,,	,,	horse
intini	,,	ఇంటిని	,,	—	,,	,,	house
kantini	,,	కంటిని	,,	—	,,	,,	eye
nōtini	,,	నోటిని	,,	—	,,	,,	mouth
chēthini	,,	చేతిని	,,	—	,,	,,	hand
kālini	,,	కాలిని	,,	—	,,	,,	leg
oorini	,,	ఊరిని	,,	—	,,	,,	village

Now, we learn about the application of the prepositional terminations in the plural number. *

āvul*u*	ఆవులు	—āvulanu ఆవులను
kandlu	కండ్లు	—kandl*a*thō కండ్లతో
gur̄r̄amulu	గుఱ్ఱములు	—gur̄r̄amul*a*meeḏa గుఱ్ఱములమీద
kākulu	కాకులు	—kākul*a*pī కాకులపై
kāl̄l̄u	కాళ్లు	—kāl̄l̄*a*thō కాళ్ళతో
chēthul*u*	చేతులు	—chēthul*a*lō చేతులలో
ool̄l̄u	ఊళ్లు	—ool̄l̄*a*nundi ఊళ్ళనుండి
manushyul*u*	మనుష్యులు	—manushyul*a*lō మనుష్యులలో
sēvukul*u*	సేవకులు	—sēvakul*a*pī సేవకులపై
chetl*u*	చెట్లు	—chetl*a*meeḏa చెట్లమీద
bāluru	బాలురు	—bālur*a*ku బాలురకు

* It is better to revise the lesson on *the plural number* before beginning the present portion.

From the examples you will find that **the last** *u* (ు) **of a noun in the plural number is changed to** *a* (✓) **before a preposition is added.** It may be mentioned here that the objective case termination in the plural number is always *nu* ను only and the English word "to" is always denoted in the plural number in Telugu by the letter *ku* కు. (*ni* ని and *ki* కి are not at all used for nouns in the plural number).

Read the following sentences :—

mēmu cinemāku pōvuc̄hunnāmu మేము సినిమాకు పోవు చున్నాము—We are going to (the) ninema

meeru kooda vaththurā మీరు కూడ వత్తురా ?—Will you also come ?

halu ikkadaku entha d̄ooramulō unnad̄i హాలు ఇక్కడకు ఎంత దూరములో ఉన్నది ?—How far is (the) hall from (to) here ?

hālu ikkadaku c̄hālā d̄ooramulō unnad̄i హాలు ఇక్కడకు చాల దూరములో ఉన్నది—(The) hall is very far from (to) here.

meeru mā bandilō randu మీరు మా బండిలో రండు—Come in our cart.

Subbannā ! bandi thvaragā thōlu సుబ్బన్నా ! బండి త్వరగా తోలు—Subbannā, drive the cart quickly.

cinemāku vēla aguc̄hunnad̄i సినిమాకు వేళ అగుచున్నది—Time for (the) cinema (show) is nearing.

roopāyi tikketlu pad̄i indu రూపాయి టిక్కెట్లు పది ఇందు—give (me) ten (one-) rupee tickets.

ivigō ticketlu theesikonudu ఇవిగో టిక్కెట్లు తీసికొనుడు—take these tickets.

hālulōniki pondu హాలు లోనికి పొండు—go into (the) hall.

mee ticketlu ekkada unnavi ? మీ టిక్కెట్లు ఎక్కడ ఉన్నవి ?—where are your tickets ?

ivigo, mā ticketlu ఇవిగో మా టిక్కెట్లు—these are our tickets.

ee kurcheelapī koorchundudu ఈ కుర్చీల పై కూర్చుండుడు—sit on these chairs.

meeru sōdā thrāgud̄urā, chā thrāgud̄urā ? మీరు సోడా త్రాగుదురా, చా త్రాగుదురా ?—will you (drink) take soda, or tea ?

nēnu sōdā thrāgud̄unu నేను సోడా త్రాగుదును—I shall take (drink) soda.

mēmu chā thrāgud̄umu మేము చా త్రాగుదుము—we shall take (drink) tea.

pillavādā, rendu sōdālu thē పిల్లవాడా రెండు సోడాలు తే—boy, get two soda (bottles).

id̄igō, chā theesikonudu ఇదిగో చా తీసికొనుడు—take this tea.

pillavādā id̄igō dabbu teesikō పిల్లవాడా, ఇదిగో డబ్బు తీసికో—boy, take this money.

aata chāla bāgugā unnad̄i ఆట చాల బాగుగా ఉన్నది—(the) show is very good.

LESSON 3

Tenses

THE PRESENT TENSE

va-c̄hc̄hu	వచ్చు	—to come	ki	కి	—to
bayalu-d̄eru	బయలుదేరు	—to start	nā	నా	—my
			kalamu	కలము	—pen
pōvu	పోవు	—to go	kā-gi-thamu	కాగితము	—paper
the-c̄hchu	తెచ్చు	—to bring	ka-chē-ree	కచేరి	} office
i-c̄hchu	ఇచ్చు	—to give	kā-rya-la-ya-mu	కార్యాలయము	} office
mō-yu	మోయు	—to carry			
pilu-c̄hu	పిలుచు	—to call	sēvakudu	సేవకుడు	—servant
vrā-yu	వ్రాయు	—to write	yajamāni	యజమాని	—officer, master
c̄ha-du-vu	చదువు	—to read			
koo-da	కూడ	—too, also	nē-nu	నేను	—I
ippudu	ఇప్పుడు	—now	mē-mu	మేము	—we
lō	లో	—in	neevu	నీవు	—thou (you)
thō	తో	—with			
meed̄a	మీద	—on	meeru	మీరు	—you
thamaru	తమరు	—you	a-di	అది	—it*

* In Telugu, "it" is used not only for lifeless things but also for birds, beasts, flies, etc.

vādu వాడు }
athadu అతడు } —he
āyana అయన }
ā-me ఆమె —she

vā-ru వారు —they (humans)
Ā-vi అవి —they (other than humans)

nēnu	pōvu	chunnanu	నేను పోవు చున్నాను	—	I am going
,,	vaC̄hchu	,,	,, వచ్చు ,,	—	,, coming
,,	theC̄hchu	,,	,, తెచ్చు ,,	—	,, bringing
,,	iC̄hchu	,,	,, ఇచ్చు ,,	—	,, giving
,,	piluC̄hu	,,	,, పిలుచ్చు ,,	—	,, calling
,,	vrāyu	,,	,, వ్రాయు ,,	—	,, writting
,,	C̄haduvu	,,	,, చదువు ,,	—	,, reading
,,	mōyu	,,	,, మోయు ,,	—	,, carrying

memu	mō-yu	C̄hunnāmu	మేము మోయు చున్నాము	—	,, We are carrying
,,	pō-vu	,,	,, పోవు ,,	—	,, going
neevu	vrā-yu	C̄hunnāvu	నీవు వ్రాయుచున్నావు	—	You(thou)are writing
,,	pō-vu	,,	,, పోవు ,,	—	,, going
,,	vaC̄hchu	,,	,, వచ్చు ,,	—	,, coming

meeru	iC̄hchu	C̄hunnaru	మీరు ఇచ్చుచున్నారు	—	,, giving
,,	piluC̄hu	,,	,, పిలుచు ,,	—	,, calling
,,	C̄haduvu	,,	,, చదువు ,,	—	,, reading
vādu	vrāyu	C̄hunnādu	వాడు వ్రాయుచున్నాడు	—	He is writing
,,	mōyu	,,	,, మోయు ,,	—	,, carrying
,,	theC̄hchu	,,	,, తెచ్చు ,,	—	,, bringing

āme C̄hād̄uvu C̄hunnadi			**అమె చదువుచున్నది**		**—She is reading**	
,,	**ichchu**	,, ,,	**ఇచ్చు**	,,	**— ,,**	**giving**
,,	**vrāyu**	,, ,,	**వ్రాయు**	,,	**— ,,**	**writing**
,,	**piluC̄hu**	,, ,,	**పిలుచు**	,,	**— ,,**	**calling**
a-d̄i pō-vu		,,	**ఆది పోవుచున్నది**		**—It is going**	
a-vi pōvu chunnavi			**అవి పోవుచున్నవి**		**—They are going**	
vāru vaC̄hchu C̄hunnaru			**వారు వచ్చుచున్నారు**		**–They are coming**	
,,	**piluchu**	,, ,,	**పిలుచు**	,,	**— ,,**	**calling**
,,	**ichchu**	,, ,,	**ఇచ్చు**	,,	**— ,,**	**giving**
,.	**thechchu**	,, ,,	**తెచ్చు**	,,	**— ,,**	**bringing**

By going through the above examples, you will understand the following points :—

(1) If "C̄hunnānu" is added to words denoting some kind of action, it gives the meaning, "I am......ing."

(2) If "chunnāmu," is added to such words, it gives the meaning, "we are......ing."

(3) If "chunnāvu" is added, it means, "you (thou) are ......ing."

(4) If "chunnāru" is added, it means, "you are......ing." or "They are...ing." (Here, *they* applies to human beings only.)

(5) If "chunnādu" is added, it means, "He is......ing."

(6) If "chunnadi" is added, it means, "It, she...is...ing"

(7) If "chunnavi" is added, it means, They are...ing"

(Here, *they* applies to subjects other than human beings.)

The words *vachchu* వచ్చు *Pōvu* పోవు etc., (given on the left at the beginning of this lesson) denote the acts of coming, and going, etc. They are called the **roots** of verbs.

The words *C̄hunnānu* చున్నాను, *C̄hunnāmu* చున్నాము, etc., are called "the Present tense **terminations**" because they are added at the end of the roots to show different persons, numbers, genders, etc., in the present tense.

These terminations are added to the roots according to the person, number and gender of the person or thing doing the action (i. e. the subject).

When the words "I" and "We" are used, the subject is said to be in the **first person**. When "you*" is used, it is in the **second person**. When other words are used it is in the **third person**.

Now, see how the abovesaid terminations are classified below in Chart No. 5.

CHART 5.

Person	Singular number.	Plural number.
1st (I, we)		
	C̄hunnānu చున్నాను	C̄hunnāmu చున్నాము
2nd (thou, you)		
	C̄hunnāvu చున్నావు	C̄hunnāru చున్నారు
3rd (He, she, it, they etc.)		
	C̄hunnāḍu చున్నాడు (male)	C̄hunnāru చున్నారు (humans)
	C̄hunnaḍi చున్నది (others)	C̄hunnāvi చున్నవి (others)

---

* When the person to whom we are speaking is a servant, child, close friend or any other person to whom no respect need be shown, the word "neevu" (నీవు = you) is used in Telugu. On the other hand, if the person spoken to is one to whom we have to show respect, we have to use "meeru" మీరు both for the singular and plural numbers,

We can now frame sentencess with the vocabulary given at the beginning of this lesson with the help of Chart No. 5.

nēnu kachēreeki pōvuchunnānu నేను కచేరీకి పోవుచున్నాను.	= I am going to (the) office.
nā sēvakudu kooda bayaludēru C̄hunnādu నా సేవకుడు కూడ బయలుదేరు చున్నాడు	= My servant also is starting.
kachēree lo nēnu vrayuchunnānu కచేరిలో నేను వ్రాయుచున్నాను	= I am writing in (the) office.
nēnu kāgithamu meed̄a vrāyu chunnānu నేను కాగితము మీద వ్రాయుచున్నాను	= I am writing on (a) paper.
nēnu nā kalamuthō vrāyuchunnānu నేను నా కలముతో వ్రాయు చున్నాను	= I am writing with my pen.
nā yajamāni piluC̄huchunnādu నా యజమాని పిలుచుచున్నాడు	= My officer is calling (me).
nēnu ippudu vaC̄huchunnānu నేను ఇప్పుడు వచ్చుచున్నాను	= I am coming now.
kagithamu pōvuchunnad̄i కాగితము పోవుచున్నది	= The paper is going (flying away)
nā sēvakudu kāgithamu theC̄hchu C̄hunnadu నా సేవకుడు కాగితము తెచ్చుచున్నాడు	= My servant is bringing (the) paper.
vādu yajamāniki kāgithamu ichuchu-chunnādu వాడు యజమానికి కాగితము ఇచ్చుచున్నాడు	= He is giving (the) paper to (the) officer.
vādu kalamu kooda ichchuchunnādu వాడు కలము కూడ ఇచ్చుచున్నాడు	= He is giving (the) pen also

nā yajamāni kāgithamu chaduvu chunnādu నా యజమాని కాగితము చదువుచున్నాడు	= My officer is reading (the) paper.
nēnu pōvuchunnanu నేను పోవుచున్నాను	= I am going.
meeru kooda vachchu chunnāru మీరు కూడ వచ్చుచున్నారు	= You are also coming.
nā sēvakudu nā kāgitamulu mōyu-chunnādu నా సేవకుడు నా కాగితములు మోయుచున్నాడు	= My servant is carrying my papers.
vāru kooda vachchuchunnāru వారు కూడవచ్చుచున్నారు	= They are also comming.
vāru kāgithamulu kooda thec̄hchu C̄hunnāru వారు కాగితములు కూడ తెచ్చుచున్నారు	= They are bringing papers also.

The student will observe from the above examples that the verb (word or words denoting the action) comes at the end of the sentence.

He will also observe that **lu** లు is added to the noun in the singular number to change it into the plural, just as **s** is added to nouns in English. Plural number in Telugu is generally formed by adding **lu** లు to a noun in the singular. See lesson on "Nouns" for details.

The present tense formations of the root "*undu* ఉండు" (to be, to stay) are as follows —

Person.	**Singular number.**	**Plural number.**
1st	unnānu ఉన్నాను —I am	unnāmu ఉన్నాము —we are
2nd	unnâvu ఉన్నావు —thou are	unnāru ఉన్నారు —you are
3rd	unnādu ఉన్నాడు —he is	unnāru ఉన్నారు —they are (for human beings only)
	unnadi ఉన్నది —she/it is	unnavi ఉన్నవి —they are (other than human beings.)

PAST TENSE

geluChu	గెలుచు—to conquer	nātinchu	నాటించు—to cause to plant-(to get something planted).
theChchu	తెచ్చు—to bring	rēpu	రేపు —to-morrow
thŌlu	తోలు—to drive	ninna	నిన్న —yesterday.
chēyu	చేయు - to do, to make	bāguga బాగుగా	—good.
kŌyu	కోయు—to cut,	mā	మా —our.
mooyu	· మూయు—to close, to shut	mee	మీ —your.
		thŌta	తోట —garden.
pŌyu	పోయు—to pour	chettu	చెట్టు —tree.
geeyu	గీయు—to draw	māmidi	మామిడి —mango.

Choopinchu చూపించు —to show

nātu నాటు—to plant

undu ఉండు— to be; to stap

thatha తాత—grandfather

kumārudu కుమారుడు—son

kumārthē కుమార్తె—daughter

gulābi poolu గులాబి పూలు—rose flowers

āru ఆరు —six.

samvathsaramu సంవత్సరము — year.

thiyyagā తియ్యగా—sweet.

kobbari chettu కొబ్బరి చెట్టు —coconut tree.

kanche కంచె—fence.

poola-mokka పూల మొక్క—flower plant.

Read the following sentences :—

nēnu vach*ithini* నేను వచ్చితిని—I came.
,, Choochi*thini* ,, చూచితిని—I saw.
,, gelichi*thini* ,, గెలిచితిని—I (conquered) won.
,, thechchi*thini* ,, తెచ్చితిని—I brought.
,, thōli*thini* ,, తోలితిని—I drove.

mēmu vachchi*thimi* మేము వచ్చితిమి—We came.
,, **Choochi*thimi*** ,, చూచితిమి—We saw.
,, **gelichi*thimi*** ,, గెలిచితిమి —We won.
,, **thechchi*thimi*** ,, తెచ్చితిమి—We brought.
,, **thōli*thimi*** ,, తోలితిమి—We drove.

neevu vachchi*thivi* నీవు వచ్చితివి —you (thou) came.
,, **Choochi*thivi*** ,, చూచితివి — ,, saw.
,, **gelichi*thivi*** ,, గెలిచితివి — ,, won.
,, **thechchi*thivi*** ,, తెచ్చితివి — ,, brought.
,, **thōli*thivi*** ,, తోలితివి — ,, drove.

meeru vachchi*thiri*	మీరు వచ్చితిరి	—you came
,, Choochi*thiri*	,, చూచితిరి	— ,, saw
,, gelichi*thiri*	,, గెలిచితిరి	— ,, won
,, thechchi*thiri*	,, తెచ్చితిరి	— ,, brought
,, thōli*thiri*	,, తోలితిరి	— ,, drove

{vādu / āme / adi / avi*} vachche*nu* {వాడు / ఆమె / అది / అవి*} వచ్చెను— {he / she / it / they*} came

,, Chooche*nu*	,, చూచెను	,,	saw
,, geliche*nu*	,, గెలిచెను	,,	won
,, thechche*nu*	,, తెచ్చెను	,,	brought
,, thōle*nu*	,, తోలెను	,,	drove

vāru vachch*iri*	వారు వచ్చిరి—	They*	came
,, chooch*iri*	,, చూచిరి—	,,	saw
,, gelich*iri*	,, గెలిచిరి—	,,	won
,, thechch*iri*	తెచ్చిరి—	,,	brought
,, thōl*iri*	తోలిరి—	,,	drove

* The word "they" (*avi*) here denotes all nouns other than human beings.

*The word "they" (*varu*) denotes here human beings.

From the above examples, we find that Past tense can be formed by adding the following terminations to the roots according to the person and number of the subjects in sentences :—

Person.		*Singular.*	*Plural.*
1st	(I, we)	ithini ఇతిని	ithimi ఇతిమి
2nd	(thou, you)	ithivi ఇతివి	ithiri ఇతిరి
3rd	(he, she it, they)	enu ఎను	iri ఇరి (for human beings) enu ఎను (for others)

While adding these terminations to the roots, you have to note one or two important points. All roots or "changed roots" (of the colloquial imperative mood) in Telugu end in a vowel. This *last* vowel is omitted when a termination *beginnings* with a vowel is added to the root or to a "changed root."

e. g.	amm*u* + *i*ri	= am*m* + iri	= ammiri
	kon*u* + *i*ri	= ko*n* + iri	= koniri
	vac̄hch*u* + *i*ri	= vachc*h* + *i*ri	= vachchiri
	c̄hooc̄h*u* + *e*nu	= c̄hooc*h* + enu	= choochenu

In all the above examples the last *u* of the root has been omitted because the termination *iri* or enu (beginning with a vowel) is added.

Now the past tense formations of two roots *ammu* అమ్ము and *kattu* కట్టు are given below as examples for the information and guidance of the student :—

ammu అమ్ము—to sell.

Person	Singular	Plural.
1st	amm*ithini* అమ్మితిని	amm*ithimi* అమ్మితిమి
2nd	amm*ithivi* అమ్మితివి	amm*ithiri* అమ్మితిరి
3rd	amm*enu* అమ్మెను	amm*iri* అమ్మిరి amm*enu* అమ్మెను

kattu కట్టు—to build.

1st	katt*ithini* కట్టితిని	katt*ithimi* ట్టితిమి
2nd	katt*ithivi* కట్టితివి	katt*ithiri* కట్టితిరి
3rd	katt*enu* కట్టెను	katt*iri* కట్టిరి katt*enu* కట్టెను

Again, see the following formations :—

Root.		Past-tense.	
ge*lu*C̄hu	గెలుచు	— ge*lichithini*	గెలిచితిని
pi*lu*C̄hu	పిలుచు	— pi*lichithiri*	పిలిచితిరి
ko*lu*C̄hu	కొలుచు	— ko*li*che*nu*	కొలిచెను
C̄ha*d̄u*vu	చదువు	— C̄ha*d̄i*ve*nu*	చదివెను

From these examples you will see that the last-but-one *u* (ు) of the roots is changed to *i* (ి) This change occurs whenever a termination beginning with *i* ఇ or *e* ఎ is added to roots having *u* (ు) as the last but one vowel.

Read the following formations and note the change.—

chē*yu*	+ *i*thini	—chē*si*thini	(**not** chē*yi*thini)
చేయు	+ ఇతిని	—చేసితిని	(**not** చేయితిని)
vrā*yu*	+ *i*thini	—vrā*si*thini	(**not** vrā*yi*thini)
వ్రాయు	+ ఇతివి	—వ్రాసితివి	(**not** వ్రాయితివి)
kō*yu*	+ *i*thivi	—kō*si*thivi	(**not** ko*yi*thivi)
కోయు	+ ఇతివి	—కోసితివి	(**not** కోయితివి)
moo*yu*	+ *i*thiri	—moo*si*thiri	(**not** moo*yi*thiri)
మూయు	+ ఇతిరి	—మూసితిరి	(**not** మూయితిరి)
pō*yu*	+ ēnu	—pōsenu	(**not** pō*y*enu)
పోయు	+ ఎను	—పోసెను	(**not** పోయెను)
gee*yu*	+ *e*nu	—geesenu	(**not** geeyenu)
గీయు	+ ఎను	—గీసెను	(**not** గీయెను)
chē*yu*	+ ēnu	—chēsenu	(**not** chéyenu)
చేయు	+ ఎను	—చేసెను	(**not** చేయెను)

From the above examples it will be seen that when a termination beginning with *i* ఇ or *e* ఎ, is added to a root ending in *yu* యు, that *yu* యు, is replaced by the letter *s* స్.

kōyu + *ithiri* = *kōs* + *ithiri* = *kōsithiri* కోయు + ఇతిరి + కోస్ + ఇతిరి + కోసితిరి.

kōyu + *enu* = kos + enu = *kōsenu* కోయు + ఎను = కోస్ + ఎను = కోసెను.

chē*yu* + *i*ri = chēs + *i*ri = chē*si*ri చేయు + ఇరి = చేస్ + ఇరి = చేసిరి.

chē*yu* + ēnu = chēs + *e*nu = chēsenu చేయు + ఎను = చేస్ + ఎను + చేసెను.

Let us now frame some sentences in the past tense :—

meeru ikkadaku eppudu vachchithiri ? మీరు ఇక్కడకు ఎప్పుడు వచ్చితిరి ?—when did you come here ?

nēnu ikkadaku ninna vachchithini నేను ఇక్కడకు నిన్న వచ్చితిని —I came here yesterday.

appudu meeru nā pusthakamu choochithirā ? అప్పుడు మీరు నా పుస్తకము చూచితిరా ? —did you then see my book ?

ounu, appudu nēnu mee pusthakamu choochithini ఔను, అప్పుడు నేను మీపుస్తకము చూచితిని - yes, I saw your book then.

adi etlu unnadi ? అది ఎట్లు వున్నది ?—how is it ?

adi chāla bāgugā unnadi అది చాల బాగుగా ఉన్నది—it is very good.

meeru mā thōta choochithirā మీరు మా తోట చూచితిరా ?—did you see our garden ?

randu, mā thōta choopinthunu రండు మా తోట చూపింతును—come, I will show (you) our garden.

ivigō, māmidi chetlu ఇవిగో, మామిడి చెట్లు—these (are) mango trees.

ee chetlu āru samvathsaramula krindata nātithimi ఈ చెట్లు ఆరు సంవత్సరముల క్రిందట నాటితిమి — (w) planted these trees six years ago.

ee poolamokkalu nā kumārudu badinundi thechchenu ఈ పూలమొక్కలు నా కుమారుడు బడినుండి తెచ్చెను—my son brought these flower-plants from (the) school.

nēnu rēpu ee thōtaku kanche nātinthunu నేను రేపు ఈ తోటకు కంచె నాటింతును — I shall get the garden fenced tomorrow.

ee chettu kāya Chāla thiyyagā undunu ఈ చెట్టు కాయ చాల తియ్యగా ఉండును—the fruit of this tree would be very sweet.

ee kobbari chetlu mā thātha nātenu ఈ కొబ్బరి చెట్లు మా తాత నాటెను—our grand-father planted these cocoanut trees.

meeru ee rendu māmidi pandlu thinudu మీరు ఈ రెండు మామిడి పండ్లు తినుడు—(please) eat these two mangoes.

ee gulābi poolu mee kumārtheku indu ఈ గులాబి పూలు మీ కుమార్తెకు ఇండు—(please) give these rose-flowers to your daughter.

SOME SPECIAL FORMATIONS

Observe the following past tense formations, which are somewhat different from the usual ones.

(1) Pōvu పోవు—to go.

Person	Singular	Plural
1st	pōyithini పోయితిని	pōyithimi పోయితిమి
2nd	pōyithivi పోయితివి	pōyithiri పోయితిరి
3rd	pōyenu పోయెను	pōyiri పోయిరి (for humans) pōyenu (for others)

Here the last consonant v వ్ (pōvu) is changed to y య్ (pōyu) before the fast tense terminations are added.

(2) agu అగు—to be; to become.

Person	Singular	Plural
1st	ayithini అయితిని	ayithimi అయితిమి
2nd	ayithivi అయితివి	ayithiri అయితిరి
3rd	ayyenu అయ్యెను	ayiri అయిరి (for human beings) ayyenu అయ్యెను (for others)

Here also, the last consonant *g* గ్ (agu) is changed to *y* య్ before the past tense terminations are added. Further, when *enu* ఎ is added, that *y* is doubled (a*yy*enu అయ్యెను).

(3) undu ఉండు—to be; to stay.

Person	Singular	Plural
1st	untini ఉంటిని	untimi ఉంటిమి
2nd	untivi ఉంటివి	untiri ఉంటిరి
3rd	undenu ఉండెను	undiri ఉండిరి (for human beings) undenu ఉండెను (for others)

Here *ndithi* ండితి is changed into *nti* ంటి. (Instead of u*ndithi*ni, ఉండితిని etc. we have u*nti*ni ఉంటిని etc.) Similar change happens also for many roots ending in *nu* ను, such as *thinu* తిను *vinu* విను (to hear), konu కొను, etc., when *nithi* నితి becomes *nti* ంటి as shown below :—

Instead of (incorrect)	**We have** (correct)
thi*nithi*ni తినితిని	thi*nti*ni తింటిని
thi*nithi*mi తినితిమి	thi*nti*mi తింటిమి
ko*nithi*vi కొనితివి	ko*nti*vi కొంటివి
ko*nithi*ri కొనితిరి	ko*nti*ri కొంటిరి
vi*nithi*mi వినితిమి	vi*nti*mi వింటిమి
vi*nithi*ri వినితిరి	vi*nti*ri వింటిరి

THE FUTURE TENSE

dukanamu దుకాణము angad̄i అంగడి	—shop	
angadi veed̄hi అంగడివీధి bazāru బజారు	—market. street	
kooragāyalu కూరగాయలు	—vegetables	
pandu పండు	—(a ripe) fruit	
pandlu పండ్లు	—ripe fruits	
gampa గంప	—basket	
vankayalu వంకాయలు	—brinjals	
bendakāyalu బెండకాయలు	lady's fingers (Ramshorn)	
māmidi pandlu మామిడిపండ్లు	—mangoes	
arati pandlu అరటి పండ్లు	—plantains	

konu కొను – to buy
ammu అమ్ము–to sell
thinu తిను –to eat
pettu పెట్టు –to put
rendu రెండు–two
moodu మూడు– three
nālugu నాలుగు–four
C̄hoppuna చొప్పున –at the rate of
manchi మంచి-good
krullina క్రుళ్ళిన – rotten
etlu ఎట్లు – how
end̄uku ఎందుకు – why

nēnu ammu*d̄unu*	నేను అమ్ముదును	— I shall sell.
,, pōvu*d̄unu*	నేను పోవుదును	— I shall go.
,, chēyu*d̄unu*	నేను చేయుదును	— I shall do.
,, mōyu*d̄unu*	నేను మోయుదును	— I shall carry.
,, vrāyu*d̄unu*	వ్రాయుదును	— I shall write.
,, C̄had̄uvu*d̄unu*	నేను చదువుదును	— I shall read.
mēmu ammu*d̄umu*	మేము అమ్ముదుము	— we shall sell.
,, pōvu*d̄umu*	మేము పోవుదుము	— we shall go.
,, chēyu*d̄umu*	మేము చేయుదుము	— we shall do.
,, mōyu*d̄umu*	మేము మోయుదుము	— we shall carry.
,, vrāyu*d̄umu*	మేము వ్రాయుదుము	— we shall write.
,, C̄had̄uvu*d̄umu*	మేము చదువుదుము	— we shall read.

neevu ammu*d̄uvu*	నీవు అమ్ముదువు	—	you (thou) will sell
,, pōvu*d̄uvu*	నీవు పోవుదువు	—	you will go.
,, chēyu*d̄uvu*	నీవు చేయుదువు	—	you will do.
,, mōyu*d̄uvu*	నీవు మోయుదువు	—	you will carry.
,, vrāyu*d̄uvu*	నీవు వ్రాయుదువు	—	you will write.
,, C̄had̄uvu*d̄uvu*	నీవు చదువుదువు	—	you will read.

meeru / vāru ammu*d̄uru*	మీరు / వారు	అమ్ముదురు —	you / they	will sell.
,, pōvu*d̄uru*	,,	పోవుదురు —	,,	will go.
,, chēyu*d̄uru*	,,	చేయుదురు —	,,	will do.
,, mōyu*d̄uru*	,,	మోయుదురు —	,,	will carry
,, vrāyu*d̄uru*	,,	వ్రాయుదురు —	,,	will write
,, C̄had̄uvu*d̄uru*	,,	చదువుదురు —	,,	will read.

vādu / āme / ad̄i / avi ammu*nu*	వాడు / ఆమె / అది / అవి	అమ్మును	He / she / it / they	will sell
,, pōvunu	,,	పోవును —	,,	will go.
,, chēyu*nu*	,,	చేయును —	,,	will do.
,, mōyu*nu*	,,	మోయును —	,,	will carry.
,, vrāyu*nu*	,,	వ్రాయును —	,,	will write.
,, C̄had̄uvu*nu*	,,	చదువును —	,,	will read.
,, C̄hooC̄hu*nu*	,,	చూచును —	,,	will see.
,, vaC̄huchu*nu*	,,	వచ్చును —	,,	will come.
,, piluC̄hu*nu*	,,	పిలుచును —	,,	will call.
,, techC̄hu*nu*	,,	తెచ్చును —	,,	will get.
,, iC̄hchu*nu*	,,	ఇచ్చును —	,,	will give.
,, konu*nu*	,,	కొనును —	,,	will buy.

You will observe the following points from studying the above examples :—

(1) If *dunu* దును is added to the roots, it gives the meaning, "I shall......"

(2) If *d̄umu* దుము is added, it means "We shall......"

(3) If *d̄uvu* దువు is added, it means, "you(thou)will..."

(4) If *d̄uru* దురు is added, it means either "You will..." or, "they (human beings) will......"

(5) If *nu* ను is added, it means, "He/she/it, or they (other than human beings) will......"

These *d̄unu* దును, *d̄umu* దుము etc., are called **the future tense terminations** † These are given below in a table form for easy reference :—

CHART 6

Person	Singular number	Plural number
1st (I, we)	*dunu* దును	*d̄umu* దుము
2nd (thou, you)	*d̄uvu* దువు	*d̄uru* దురు
3rd (he, she, it, they etc.)	nu ను	*d̄uru* దురు (for humans) nu ను (for others)

Before beginning to frame sentences in this (future) tense, we have to note one or two points more.

As you have already seen, chēyu చేయు + d̄unu దును = చేయుదును chēyudunu.

† There is another set of terminations for the future tense and it will be dealt with later on to avoid confusion and congestion.

mōyu మోయు + d̄unu దును = మోయుదును mōyud̄unu

Here there is no change at all in the letters of the word (verb) formed by adding the termination to the root. But, see the following words :—

piluc̄hu పిలుచు + d̄unu దును = piluthunu పిలుతును

c̄hooc̄hu చూచు + d̄uru దురు = c̄hoothuru చూతురు

Thus, c̄hu చు + d̄u దు has become *thu* తు

Again,

vac̄hchu వచ్చు + d̄umu దుము = vaththumu వత్తుము

thec̄hchu తెచ్చు + d̄uvu దువు = theththuvu తెత్తువు

ic̄hchu ఇచ్చు + d̄unu దును = iththunu ఇత్తును

Thus, c̄hchu చ్చు + d̄u దు has become ththu త్తు.

From the above examples we can see that

(1) whenever a root ending in *chu* చు is joined by a termination beginning with d̄u దు, *thu* తు comes in the place of *chu d̄u* చు దు, and

(2) whenever a root ending in *chchu* చ్చు is joined by a terminations beginning with d̄u దు, *ththu* త్తు takes the place of c̄hchud̄u చ్చుదు.

These two points are to be remembered well to avoid incorrect writing. See the following examples also:–

piluc̄hu పిలుచు + d̄umu దుము – piluthumu పిలుతుము we shall call

,, + d̄uru దురు — piluthuru పిలుతురు you/they will call

C̄hooC̄hu చూచు + d̄unu దును = choothunu చూతును I shall see.
,, + d̄umu దుము = C̄hoothumu చూతుము we shall see.
,, + d̄uvu దువు = C̄hoothuvu చూతువు you shall see.
VaC̄hchu వచ్చు + d̄unu దును = Vaththunu వత్తును I shall come.
,, + d̄uvu దువు = Vaththuvu వత్తువు you (thou) will come.
,, + d̄uru దురు = Vaththuru వత్తురు you/they will come.
iC̄hchu ఇచ్చు + d̄umu దుము = iththumu ఇత్తుము we shall give
,, + d̄uvu దువు = iththuvu ఇత్తువు you (thou) will give.
,, + d̄uru దురు = iththuru ఇత్తురు you/they will give.
thechchu తెచ్చు + d̄unu దును = theththunu తెత్తును I shall get.
,, + d̄umu దుము = theththumu తెత్తుము we shall get.
,, + d̄uru దురు = theththuru తెత్తురు you/they will get.

writing the above words as piluC̄hud̄amu పిలుచెదము, piluC̄huduru పిలుచెదురు, C̄hooC̄hudunu చూచెదను vaC̄hchud̄unu వచ్చెదను, iC̄hchud̄umu ఇచ్చెదము etc., is *incorrect*.

Read the following sentences :—

manamu pōvu*da*mu మనము పోవుదము — *Let us* go.
,, chēyu*da*mu ,, చేయుదము — *Let us* do.
,, mōyu*da*mu ,, మోయుదము — *Let us* carry.
,, kattu*da*mu ,, కట్టుదము — *Let us* build.

manamu choo*tha*mu మనము చూతము—*Let us* **see.**

,, lē*tha*mu ,, లేతము —*Let us* **get up.**

,, va*th*'*tha*mu ,, వత్తము —*Let us* **come.**

From the above words, we can see that by removing the last-but-one vowel *u* from the first person plural formations of the future tense, we get the meaning "let us do".

(This is almost the imperative mood in the first person). Again read the following sentences :—

Pōvu*d̄a*mā ? పోవుదమా ? — shall we go ?
chēyu*d̄a*mā? చేయుదమా? — shall we do ?
mōyu*d̄a*mā? మోయుదమా?— shall we carry ?
kattu*d̄a*mā ? కట్టుదమా ? — shall we build ?
choo*tha*mā ? చూతమా ? — shall we see ?
lē*tha*mā ? లేతమా ? — shall we rise ?
va*th*tha*ma*ā ? వత్తమా ? — shall we come ?

In the above sentences, the speaker is asking the second person whether **both of them** may go, do, carry etc. Not only mere future but desire is understood from these formations.

The following special formations of the future tense are to be noted carefully :—

(1) ఉండు **Undu**—to be

person	singular	plural
1st	und̄unu ఉందును	und̄umu ఉందుము
2nd	und̄uvu ఉందువు	und̄uru ఉందురు
3rd	undunu ఉండును	und̄uru ఉందురు (for human beings)
		undunu ఉండును (other than human beings).

(2) కలుగు **kalugu**—to be

	singular	*plural*
1st person	**Kalanu** కలను	Kalamu కలము
2nd ,,	**Kalavu** కలవు	Kalaru కలరు
3rd ,,	**Kaladu** కలడు **(for a male)**	Kalaru కలరు (for human beings)
	Kalad̄u కలదు **(other than a male)**	Kalavu కలవు (other than human beings.)

Now, read the following sentences :—

meeru ekkadaku pŌvuČhunnāru మీరు ఎక్కడకు పోవుచున్నారు ? —where are you going?

nēnu bazāruku pŌvuČhunnānu నేను బజారుకు పోవుచున్నాను— I am going to the market.

nēnu koodā vaththunu నేను కూడా వత్తును—I shall also come.

meeru akkada ēmi konud̄uru / kond̄uru * మీరు అక్కడ ఏమి కొనుదురు ?* / కొందురు —what will you buy there?

nēnu akkada kooragāyalu, pandlu kond̄unu నేను అక్కడ కూరగాయలు, పండ్లు కొందును— I shall buy vegetables (and) fruits there.

---

* **In many** roots ending in *nu* ను this *nu* ను, is **changed usually** to *n* (O) when a termination beginning **with** *d̄u* దు is added. Thus, *konud̄uru* కొనుదురు is generally **changed to** *kond̄uru* కొందురు. *thinud̄uvu* తినుదువు is changed **to** *thind̄uvu* తిందువు, etc., etc.,

mee sēvakudu kooda bazāruku vac̄hchunā మీ సేవకుడు కూడ బజారుకు వచ్చునా?—will your servant also come to (the) market?

ounu, nā sēvakudu kooda bazāruku vac̄hchunu ఔను, నా సేవకుడు కూడ బజారుకు వచ్చును—yes, my servant also will come to (the) market.

bendakāyalu etlu ic̄hchuchunnāvu బెండకాయలు ఎట్లు ఇచ్చుచున్నావు?— how (at what price) are (you) giving lady's fingers ?

bendakāyalu sēru nālugu anālu బెండకాయలు శేరు నాలుగు అణాలు—(I am giving) lady's fingers (at) four annās (a) seer.

manchi bendakāyalu oka sēru iththuvā మంచి బెండకాయలు ఒక శేరు ఇత్తువా ?— will (you) give (me) (a) seer of good lady's fingers ?

nēnu vankāyalu kond̄unu నేను వంకాయలు కొందును— I shall buy brinjals.

rendu sērlu vankāyalu iththuvā రెండు శేర్లు వంకాయలు ఇత్తువా? —shall I give two seers (of brinjals ?

mee sēvakudu kooragāyalu gampalō pettuc̄hunnādu మీ సేవకుడు కూరగాయలు గంపలో పెట్టుచున్నాడు—your servant is putting (the) vegetables in (the) basket.

meeru ēmi pandlu konuc̄hunnāru మీరు ఏమి పండ్లు కొనుచున్నారు ?—what fruit are you buying ?

nēnu māmidi pandlu konuc̄hunnānu నేను మామిడిపండ్లు కొనుచున్నాను—I am buying mango fruit.

ee d̄ukānamulō māmidi pandlu unnavā ఈ దుకాణములో మామిడిపండ్లు ఉన్నవా ?— are (there) mangoes in this shop ?

ounu, ikkada māmidi pandlu unnavi ఔను, ఇక్కడ మామిడి పండ్లు ఉన్నవి—yes, (there) are mangoes here.

neevu arati pandlu kooda ammuduvā * నీవు అరటి పండ్లు కూడ అమ్ముదువా ?*—do you sell plantains also ?

ounu, nēnu arati pandlu kooda ammudunu ఔను, నేను అరటి పండ్లు కూడ అమ్ముదును—yes, I sell plantains also.

arati pandlu etlu iththuvu అరటి పండ్లు ఎట్లు ఇత్తువు ?—how (at what price) will you give plantains ?

manchi aratipandlu roopāyaku dajanu choppuna iththunu మంచి అరటిపండ్లు రూపాయకు డజను చొప్పున ఇత్తును — I shall give good plantains at (one) rupee (per) dozen.

ee krullina pandu kooda enduku ichchuchunnāvu ఈ కుళ్ళిన పండుకూడ ఎందుకు ఇచ్చుచున్నావు ?— why are (you) giving this rotten fruit also ?

ee manchi pandu iththunu ఈ మంచిపండు ఇత్తును—I shall give this good fruit.

mee kooragāyalu, pandlu kooda nā sēvakudu gampalō pettuchunnādu మీ కూరగాయలు పండ్లు కూడ నా సేవకుడు గంపలో పెట్టుచున్నాడు—My servant is putting your vegetables (and) fruits also in (the) basket.

athadu ā gampanu mōyunu అతడు ఆ గంపను మోయును—He will carry the basket.

---

* In English, present Indefinite tense is used to denote the future tense also. In Telugu, future tense is used to denote present Indefinite tense also.

ANOTHER USE OF THE FUTURE TENSE.

Upto now, you have learnt how to form verbs in the future tense with the help of the terminations given in the previous lesson. In Telugu, this set of terminations are used not only to denote mere future tense, but also to tell about events which are natural and/or which occur usually. See the following examples :

āvu pālu iC̄hchunu ఆవు పాలు ఇచ్చును — (The) cow gives milk.

Sooryudu thoorpuna ud̄ayinC̄hunu సూర్యుడు తూర్పున ఉదయించును — (The) sun rises in (the) east.

Pilli elukalanu C̄hampunu పిల్లి ఎలుకలను చంపును—(The) cat kills (the) rats.

In the following exercise, many such sentences are given.

EXERCISE

āvu	ఆవు	— cow
Pālu	పాలు	— milk
janthuvu	జంతువు	— animal
Pillalu	పిల్లలు	— children
Ped̄d̄avāru	పెద్దవారు	— adults
ad̄i	అది	— it
manaku	మనకు	— (to) us
Perugu	పెరుగు	— curd
C̄halla	చల్ల	— butter milk
gaddi	గడ్డి	— grass

pakshi	పక్షి	—bird
purugulu	పురుగులు	—worms
vastuvulu	వస్తువులు	—things
thrāgu	త్రాగు	—to drink
chedu	చెడు	—bad, rotten
manchi	మంచి	—good
upayōgakaramagu	ఉపయోగకరమగు	—useful
thiyyagā	తియ్యగా	—sweet (adverb)
nallagā	నల్లగా	—black ,,
thellagā	తెల్లగా	—white ,,
kooda	కూడ	—also, too

Kāki కాకి The Crow.

kāki nallagā undunu కాకి నల్లగా ఉండును— (The) crow is black.

kāni adi upayōgakaramagu pakshi కాని అది ఉపయోగకరమగు పక్షి—But, it (is) (an) useful bird.

adi purugulanu thinunu అది పురుగులను తినును—It eats (the) worms.

adi chedu vasthuvulu kooda thinunu అది చెడువస్తువులు కూడ తినును—It eats rotten things also.

Āvu ఆవు The Cow.

āvu manchi janthuvu ఆవు మంచి జంతువు— (The) cow **(is a)** good animal.

adi manaku pālu ichchunu అది మనకు పాలు ఇచ్చును—**It gives** us milk.

pillalu pālu thrāguduru పిల్లలు పాలు త్రాగుదురు— **children** drink milk.

peddavāru kooda pālu thrāguduru పెద్దవారుకూడ **పాలు** త్రాగుదురు—Adults also drink milk.

pālu thiyyagā undunu పాలు తియ్యగా ఉండును—**Milk is sweet.** avi thellagā undunu అవి తెల్లగా ఉండును—**It is white.**

pālathō perugu chēyuduru పాలతో పెరుగు చేయుదురు—**(They)** make curd with milk.

peruguthō challa chēyuduru పెరుగుతో చెల్ల చేయుదురు-**(They)** make buttermilk with curd.

challa kooda thiyyagā undunu చల్ల కూడ తియ్యగా ఉండును —butter-milk also is sweet.

āvu gaddi thinunu ఆవు గడ్డి తినును—The cow eats grass.

nēnu āvu pālu thrāguchunnānu నేను ఆవు పాలు త్రాగుచున్నాను —I am drinking cow's milk.

neevu kooda āvu pālu thrāgedavā నీవు కూడ ఆవుపాలు త్రాగెదవా?—will you also drink cow's milk?

ounu, nēnu kooda āvu pālu thrāgudunu ఔను, నేను కూడ ఆవుపాలు త్రాగుదును—yes, I also drink cow's milk.

LESSON 4

Interrogatory Sentences

ounu		—yes	kaladu	కలదు	—(she / it) is
eppudu	ఎప్పుడు	—when	unnadi	ఉన్నది	
ekkada	ఎక్కడ	—where	kalavu	కలవు	—(they) are
ekkadaku	ఎక్కడకు	—to where	unnavi	ఉన్నవి	
evaru	ఎవరు	—who	unnādu	ఉన్నాడు	—(he) is
ēmi	ఏమి	—what	kaludu	కలడు	
ēmiti	ఏమిటి		chēyu	చేయు	—to do, to make
evarini	ఎవరిని	—whom	c̄hooc̄hu	చూచు	—to see
nannu	నన్ను	—me	ā	ఆ	—the, that those (adj)
kurchee	కుర్చీ	—chair			
gad̄i	గది	—room	ee	ఈ	—this, these (adj)
chāvadi	చావడి	—Verandha	akkada	అక్కడ	—there
bhārya	భార్య	—wife	ikkada	ఇక్కడ	—here
uththaramu	ఉత్తరము	—letter	oka	ఒక	—a, one.

nēnu vac̄hchu c̄hunnanu — I am coming.
నేను వచ్చుచున్నాను

nēnu vaChchu chunnā**na** ? నేను వచ్చుచున్నానా ?	—Am I coming
neevu pŌvuChunna**vu** నీవు పోవుచున్నావు	—You are going.
neevu pŌvu Chunnā**vā** ? నీవు పోవుచున్నావా ?	—Are you going
vadu piluchu Chunnā**du** వాడు పిలుచుచున్నాడు	—He is calling.
vādu piluChuChunnā**da** ? వాడు పిలుచుచున్నాడా ?	—Is he calling ?
mēmu ChaDuvu Chunnamu మేము చదవుచున్నాము	—We are reading.
mēmu ChaDuvu Chunna**ma** ? మేము చదువుచున్నామా ?	—Are we reading ?
meeru mŌyuchunna**ru** మీరు మోయుచున్నారు	—You are carrying.
meeru mŌyuchunna**ra** ? మీరు మోయుచున్నారా ?	—Are you carrying?
vāru bayaluDeru chunna**ru** వారు బయలుదేరుచున్నారు	—They are starting.
vāru bayalu Dēruchunnā**ra** ? వారు బయలుదేరు చున్నారా ?	—Are they starting.
Āme vrāyu chunnāDi ఆమె వ్రాయుచున్నది	—She is writing.
Āme vrāyu chunnaDa ? అమె వ్రాయుచున్నదా ?	—Is she writing ?

From the foregoing examples, it will be seen that a sentence is changed to the question (interrogative) form by adding the sound ā ఆ through the short sign ా, to the last letter of the verb.

Another kind of interrogative sentence can be formed by putting one of the questioning words meaning *who, when, where why, whom, how, what, which* etc., just before the verb. See the following examples :—

evaru piluchu chunnaru ? ఎవరు పిలుచుచున్నారు ?	—who is calling ?
vadu enduku piluchu chunnādu ? వాడు ఎందుకు పిలుచుచున్నాడు ?	—why is he calling ?
Āme ekkadaku pōvuchunnadi ? ఆమె ఎక్కడకు పోవుచున్నది ?	—(To) where is she going ?
vāru etlu mōyu chunnāru ? వారు ఎట్లు మోయుచున్నారు ?	—How are they carrying ?
meeru evarini piluchu chunnāru ? మీరు ఎవరిని పిలుచుచున్నారు ?	—whom are you calling ?

Here note that it is **not** necessary to add (ā) ా to the last letter of the verb when a question/- word such as *who, why*, etc. is used in a sentence,

Now, go through the following examples and observe how interrogative sentences are formed :—

meeru ekkadaku pōvuchunnāru ? మీరు ఎక్కడకు పోవుచున్నారు ?	—where are you going ?
nenu kachēreeki pōvuchunnānu నేను కచేరికి పోవుచున్నాను..	—I am going to (the) office.
mee sēvakudu kooda bayaludēru chunnādā ? మీ సేవకుడు కూడ బయలుదేరుచున్నాడా ?	—Is your servant also starting ?

---

* Adverbs generally come before the verb in Telugu sentences.

ounu, nā sēvakudu kooda bayalu d̄eruC̄hunnādu ఔను, నా సేవకుడుకూడబయలుదేరుచున్నాడు	—yes, my servant also is starting.
meeeru kachēreelō ēmi chēyu-chuunāru ? మీరు కచేరీలో ఏమి చేయుచున్నారు ?	—what are you doing in (the) office?
nēnu kachēreelō vrāyuchunnānu నేను కచేరీలో వ్రాయుచున్నాను	—I am writing in the office.
mee yajamāni evarini piluC̄hu-C̄hunnādu ? మీ యజమాని ఎవరిని పిలుచుచున్నాడు ?	—whom is your officer calling ?
nā yajamāni nannu piluC̄hu-C̄hunnādu నా యజమాని నన్ను పిలుచుచున్నాడు	—my offlcer is calling me.
mee kāgithamulu evaru theC̄hchu-C̄hunnāru ? మీ కాగితములు ఎవరు తెచ్చుచున్నారు ?	—who is bringing your papers ?
nā kāgithamulu nā sēvakudu theC̄hchu C̄hunnādu నా కాగితము లు నా సేవకుడు తెచ్చుచున్నాడు	—My servant is bringing my papers.
mee yajamāni ekkada unnādu ? మీ యజమాని ఎక్కడ ఉన్నాడు ?	—where is your officer ?
nā yajamāni ā gad̄ilō unnādu నా యజమాని ఆ గదిలో ఉన్నాడు	—My officer is in that room.
Āyana ā gad̄ilō ēmi chēyu-C̄hunnādu ? ఆయన ఆ గదిలో ఏమి చేయుచున్నాడు ?	—what is he doing in that room ?
Āyana akkada kāgithamulu C̄hooC̄hu C̄hunnādu ఆయన అక్కడ కాగితములు చూచుచున్నాడు	—He is seeing papers there.

Āyana kurcheemeed̄a unnªdā ? ఆయన కుర్చీమీద ఉన్నాడా ?	—Is he on the chair?
ounu, āyana kurcheemeed̄a unnād̄u ఔను, ఆయన కుర్చీమీద ఉన్నాడు ?	—yes, he is on (in) the chair.
mee sēvakudu ekkad̄a unnādu ? మీ సేవకుడు ఎక్కడ ఉన్నాడు ?	—where is your servant ?
vādu ā chāvadilō unnādu వాడు ఆ చావడిలో ఉన్నాడు	—He is in that verandha.
mee kāgithamulu ekkada unnavi ? మీ కాగితములు ఎక్కడ ఉన్నవి ?	—where are your papers ?
nª kāgithamulu ee gad̄ilō unnavi నా కాగితములు ఈ గదిలో ఉన్నవి.	—my papers are in this room.
ippudu evaru vac̄hchu c̄hunnāru ? ఇప్పుడు ఎవరు వచ్చుచున్నారు ?	—who is coming now ?
ippudu nā yajamāni bhārya vac̄hchu c̄hunnad̄i ఇప్పుడు నా యజమానిభార్య వచ్చుచున్నది.	—my officer's wife is coming now.
ªme ēmi thec̄hchu c̄hunnad̄i ? ఆమె ఏమి తెచ్చుచున్నది ?	—what is she bringing ?
ªme oka kalamu thec̄hchu-c̄hunnad̄i ఆమె ఒక కలము తెచ్చుచున్నది.	—she is bringing a pen.
ªme ēmi c̄hēyu c̄hunnad̄i ? ఆమె ఏమి చేయుచున్నది ?	—what is she doing?
āme oka uththaramu vrªyu-c̄hunnad̄i ఆమె ఒక ఉత్తరము వ్రాయుచున్నది.	—she is writing a letter.

LESSON 5

Number

6. THE PLURAL NUMBER.

kooli vādu	కూలివాడు	—a cooly.	enni	ఎన్ని	—how many.
ed̄d̄u	ఎద్దు	—bullock,ox.	kroththa	క్రొత్త	–new.
bāta	బాట	—way,road.	mor̄ugu	మొఱుగు	–to bark.
gurramu	గుఱ్ఱము	—horse.	unnāru	ఉన్నారు	—(you) are (they)
kukka	కుక్క	—dog.	mellagā	మెల్లగా	—slowly.
polamu	పొలము	—field.	vadigā	వడిగా	—fast.
dabbū	డబ్బు	—money	C̄hāla	చాల	—very, many.
illu	ఇల్లు	—house.			

and̄uchē అందుచే
and̄uchētha అందుచేత
and̄uvalana అందువలన
} —Therefore.

We have already given the general rule that the plural form of a noun is got by adding *lu* లు to the singular, as,

kalamu కలము ; kalamulu కలములు—Pens.

kurchee కుర్చీ ; kurcheelu కుర్చీలు—chairs.

kāgithamu కాగితము ; kāgithamulu కాగితములు—Papers.
etc., etc.,

The following examples provide some exceptions to the above general rule :—

(a) chēyi చేయి ; chēthulu చేతులు—hands.

nooyi నూయి ; noothulu నూతులు—wells.

gōyi గోయి ; gōthulu గోతులు—Pits.

(b) rāyi రాయి ; raḻḻu రాళ్ళు—stones.

(c) vēyi వేయి : vēlu వేలు—thousands.

(d) magadu మగడు : magalu మగలు—husbands.

manusyudu మనుష్యుడు : manusyulu మనుష్యులు—men.

sīnikudu సైనికుడు : sīnikulu సైనికులు—soldiers.

(e) badi బడి : badulu బడులు—schools.

dāri దారి : dārulu దారులు—ways.

chevi చెవి : chevulu చెవులు—ears.

bāvi బావి : bāvulu బావులు—wells.

pakshi పక్షి : pakshulu పక్షులు—birds.

(f) bandi బండి : bandlu బండ్లు—carts.

buddi బుడ్డి : budlu బుడ్లు—bottles.

pandu పండు : pandlu పండ్లు—fruits.

goddu గొడ్డు : godlu గొడ్లు—cattle.

bantu బంటు : bantlu బంట్లు—servants.

sāri సారి : sārlu సార్లు—times.

pēru పేరు : pērlu పేర్లు—names.

illu ఇల్లు : indlu ఇండ్లు—houses.

eddu ఎద్దు : edlu ఎడ్లు—bullocks, oxen.

LESSON 6

Imperatives

balla	బల్ల	— table, bench
pusthakamu	పుస్తకము	— book
pāṭthamu	పాఠము	— lesson
mukhamu	ముఖము	— face
batta	బట్ట	— cloth
annamu	అన్నము	— food
vēla	వేళ	— time
badi	బడి	— school
pāṭthasāla	పాఠశాల	— school
koolivādu	కూలివాడు	— cooli, labourer
inkanu	ఇంకను	— still
bāgugā	బాగుగా	— well
nadụC̄hu	నడుచు	— to walk
niluC̄hu	నిలుచు	— to stand
viruC̄hu	విరుచు	— to break (a stick etc.)
grahinC̄hu	గ్రహించు	— to understand
prēminC̄hu	ప్రేమించు	— to love
kshaminC̄hu	క్షమించు	— to pardon
rakshinC̄hu	రక్షించు	—to save,to protect
lēC̄hu	లేచు	— to rise, to get up
agu	అగు	— to be, to become
C̄haC̄hchu	చచ్చు	— to die
koorC̄hundu	కూర్చుండు	— to sit
theesikonu	తీసికొను	— to take
nidrapōvu	నిద్రపోవు	— to sleep
kadugu	కడుగు	— to wash

ā kāgithamu meeda vrāyumu ఆ కాగితము మీద వ్రాయుము—write on that paper.

ee pusthakamu čhaduvumu ఈ పుస్తకము చదువుము—Read this book.

ā pani chēyumu ఆ పని చేయుము—Do that work.

ee pandu thinumu ఈ పండు తినుము—Eat this fruit,

thvaragā bayaludērumu త్వరగా బయలు దేరుము–start quickly.

ee gampa mōyumu ఈ గంప మోయుము—carry this basket.

ee pandlu gampalō pettumu ఈ పండ్లు గంపలో పెట్టుము—put these fruits in (the) basket.

In the above sentences, we are **telling only one person** to do certain work. Here the verb is formed by adding **mu** ము to the root.

vrāyu	+ mu—	వ్రాయుము	—write.
čhaduvu	+ mu—	చదువుము	—Read.
chēyu	+ mu—	చేయుము	—Do.
	etc.,	etc.,	

When we tell two or more persons at the some time to do certain work, **du** డు is added to the root instead of **mu** ము.

vrāyu	+du—	వ్రాయుడు—	write.
čhaduvu	+du—	చదువుడు	—Read.
chēyu	+du—	చేయుడు	—Do.

Whenever we request, advise, or order a person or persons to do or not to do something, the verb in the relative sentence is said to be in the imperative mood, All the verbs in the above examples are in this mood.

Some roots change their forms before adding *mu* ము, or *du* డు, in the Imperative mood, as,

Root		**+ mu ము**		**+ du డు**	
koluC̄hu	కొలుచు	koluvumu	కొలువుము	koluvudu	కొలువుడు
geluC̄hu	గెలుచు	geluvumu	గెలువుము	geluvudu	గెలువుడు
naduC̄hu	నడుచు	naduvumu	నడువుము	naduvudu	నడువుడు
niluC̄hu	నిలుచు	niluvumu	నిలువుము	niluvudu	నిలువుడు
piluC̄hu	పిలుచు	piluvumu	పిలువుము	piluvudu	పిలువుడు
vir̄uC̄hu	విఱుచు	vir̄uvumu	విఱువుము	vir̄uvudu	విఱువుడు
etc.		etc.		etc.	
grahinC̄hu	గ్రహించు	grahimpumu	గ్రహింపుము	grahimpudu	గ్రహింపుడు
prēminC̄hu	ప్రేమించు	prēmimpumu	ప్రేమింపుము	prēmimpudu	ప్రేమింపుడు
kshaminC̄hu	క్షమించు	kshamimpumu	క్షమింపుము	kshamimpudu	క్షమింపుడు
rakshimC̄hu	రక్షించు	rakshimpumu	రక్షింపుము	rakshimpudu	రక్షింపుడు
ādinC̄hu	ఆడించు	ādimpumu	ఆడింపుము	ādimpudu	ఆడింపుడు
thalanC̄hu	తలంచు	thalampumu	తలంపుము	thalampudu	తలంపుడు
etc.		etc.		etc.	
āgu	ఆగు	kammu	కమ్ము	kandu	కండు
iC̄hchu	ఇచ్చు	immu	ఇమ్ము	indu	ఇండు
chaC̄hchu	చచ్చు	C̄hāvumu	చావుము	C̄hāvudu	చావుడు
choochu	చూచు	C̄hoodumu	చూడుము	C̄hoodudu	చూడుడు
theC̄hchu	తెచ్చు	themmu	తెమ్ము	thendu	తెండు
pōvu	పోవు	pommu	పొమ్ము	pondu	పొండు
vaC̄hchu	వచ్చు	rammu	రమ్ము	randu	రండు
lēC̄hu	లేచు	lemmu	లెమ్ము	lendu	లెండు

From the foregoing examples, we find that before adding *mu* ము or *du* డు, the last letter of the roots ending in (a) *c̄hu* చు is changed to *vu* వు; and

(b) *nc̄hu* ంచు is changed to *mpu* ంపు.

We also find that the formations in group (c) are irregular and no hard and fast rule can be laid down for those roots.

Even in the case of (a) and (b) above, there are many exceptions which are to be learnt by observation only.

Now read the following sentences addressed to a student :—

Pillavādā! * ikkadaku rammu పిల్లవాడా! ఇక్కడకు రమ్ము —Boy, come here.

ee balla meeda koorc̄hundumu ఈ బల్ల మీద కూర్చుండుము —Sit (down) on this bench.

ā pusthakamu theesikonumu ఆ పుస్తకము తీసికొనుము —Take that book.

oka pātthamu c̄haduvumu ఒక పాఠము చదువుము—Read a lesson.

pusthakamu akkada pettumu పుస్తకము అక్కడ పెట్టుము —Put (the) book there.

---

* when calling a person, change the last vowel of the word denoting his name profession, or relationship as follows :—

(1) i ఇ to ee ఈ as, thalli తల్లి; thallee తల్లీ; Hari హరి; Haree హరీ:

(2) *a* అ & u ఉ to ā ా, as amma అమ్మ; ammā అమ్మా; bāludu బాలుడు; bāludā బాలుడా! etc—In the plural, *lu* లు becomes lārā లారా; as annalu అన్నలు; annalārā అన్నలారా.

Pillalārā! meeru inkanu nidra pōvuchunnārā? పిల్లలారా! మీరు ఇంకను నిద్రపోవుచున్నారా?—**Children,** are you still sleeping?

lendu mukhamulu kadugudu లెండు ముఖములు కడుగుడు —get up, wash (your) faces.

manchi battalu kattudu మంచి బట్టలు కట్టుడు—**wear** fresh clothes (Dress up yourselves).

pusthakamulu theesikonudu పుస్తకములు తీసికొనుడు— Take (your) books.

pātthamulu chaduvudu పాఠములు చేదువుడు—**Read** (your) lessons.

thvaragā annamu thinudu త్వరగా అన్నము తినుడు— Take (Eat) your food quickly.

vēlaku pātthasālaku pondu వేళకు పాఠశాలకు పొందు— go to school (in) time.

pātthasālalō pātthamulu bāgugā nērchukonudu పాఠశాలలో పాఠములు బాగుగా నేర్చుకొనుడు—Learn (your) lessons well in (the) school.

sāyamkalamu ādukonudu సాయంకాలము ఆడుకొనుడు— Play (in the) evening.

We have already seen that some roots change their form before *mu* ము or *du* డు are added to get the verbs in the Imperative mood. These changed forms (without the letters *mu* ము or *du* డు) may be called the "*changed* *roots.*" These "*changed roots*" are *very important* as they are used very widely in Telugu. * These are used not only in forming the passive voice, the negative, and many other miscellaneous verbal forms, but also as verbs in the *colloquial Imperative mood*, while speaking to a person such as a servant, an youngster, etc, to whom no respect need be shown †. The student is once more reminded of the importance of these *changed roots* and is advised to go through the following examples very carefully :—

	Original Root	**Changed Root**
(a)	piluChu పిలుచు	piluvu పిలువు
	naduChu నడచు	naduvu నడువు
	koluChu కొలుచు	koluvu కొలువు
	etc.	etc.
(b)	grahinChu గ్రహించు	grahimpu గ్రహింపు
	âdinChu ఆడించు	âdimpu ఆడింపు
	thalanChu తలంచు	thalampu తలంపు
	rakshinChu రక్షించు	rakshimpu రక్షింపు
	kshaminChu క్షమించు	kshamimpu క్షమింపు
	etc.	etc.

---

* These usages are dealt with in this book later on.

† The colloquial Imperative mood is used only in singular. There is no plural for it.

(c) C̄hooC̄hu	చూచు	C̄hoodu	చూడు
ĊhaC̄hchu	చచ్చు	C̄havu	చావు
etc.		etc.	

Note the changed root very carefully in the following six cases :—

Original Root		**Changed Root**	
agu	అగు	kā	కా
iC̄hchu	ఇచ్చు	(ee ఈ) * eeyu	ఈయు
theC̄hchu	తెచ్చు	thē	తే
pōvu	పోవు	pō	పో
vaC̄hchu	వచ్చు	rā	రా
lēchu	లేచు	(lē లే) * lēvu	లేవు

The verbs in the following sentences are in the colloquial Imperative mood, used only when speaking to a servant, child, etc :—

Ō koolivādā! lē, ikkadaku rā ఓ కూలివాడా! లే, ఇక్కడకు రా— o coolie ! get up, come here.

ee balla akkada pettu ఈ బల్ల అక్కడ పెట్టు—put this table there.

ā pusthakamu thē ఆ పుస్తకము తే– get that book.

thvaragā bazāruku pō త్వరగా బజారుకు పో—go to (the) market quickly.

ā gampa ikkada pettu ఆ గంప ఇక్కడ పెట్టు—Put that basket here.

ā kooragāyalu balla meed̄a pettu ఆ కూరగాయలు బల్లమీద పెట్టు—Put (keep) those vegetables on (the) table.

* These forms (shown within brackets) are used only in the colloquial Imperative mood and not in any other verbal formations.

LESSON 7

Negatives

āYlasyamu ఆలస్యము—delay.

āta sthalamu ఆటస్థలము
—playground

pand̄emu పందెము—match

pani పని—work, business.

thammudu తమ్ముడు—younger brother.

kumārudu కుమారుడు—son

nēdu నేడు—today

nāyana నాయన—father

godugu గొడుగు—umbrella

ayithē అయితే—if (so)

vērē వేరే—another, separate

konchemu కొంచెము—some; a little.

manchid̄i మంచిది—well.

lēd̄u లేదు } no,
kād̄u కాదు } not.

vad̄d̄u వద్దు } don't
valadu వలదు } don't

lēnu లే—I am not / was not

lēmu లేము—we are not / were not

lēvu లే—you are not / were

lēru లేరు—you are not / they were not

lēdu లేడు—he is not / was not

lēd̄u లేదు—she is not / it was not

lēvu లేవు—they are not / were not

Read the following sentences :—

nēnu pōvu*talēd̄u* నేను పోవుట లేదు—I am *not* going.
meeru čhad̄uvu*talēd̄u* మీరు చదువుటలేదు—you are *not* *reading*. vādu vačhchu*talēd̄u* వాడు వచ్చుటలేదు—He is *not* com*ing*.

Again, read the following sentences ;—

nēnu thina*lēdu* నేను తినలేదు—I *did not* eat.

meeru čhaduva*lēdu* మీరు చేదువలేదు—you *did not* read.

vādu čhood*alēdu* వాడు చూడలేదు—He *did not* see.

āme rā*lēdu* ఆమె రాలేదు—she *did not* come,

mēmu pō*lēdu* మేము పోలేదు—we *did not* go.

sēvakudu thē*lēdu* సేవకుడు తేలేదు—(the) servant *did not* get.

neevu piluva*lēdu* నీవు పిలువలేదు—you *did not* call.

nēnu grahimpa*lēdu* నేను గ్రహింపలేదు—I *did not* understand.

āme prēmimpa*lēdu* ఆమె ప్రేమింపలేదు—she *did not* love.

vādu naduv*alēdu* వాడు నడవలేదు—He *did not* walk.

mēmu vrāy*alēdu* మేము వ్రాయలేదు—we *did not* write.

meeru lēv*alēdu* మీరు లేవలేదు—you *did not* rise.

From the examples, it will be seen that the **negative in the past tense is formed by adding** *a lēdu* అ లేదు **to the "changed roots" (Verbs in the colloquial Imperative mood), after removing the last** *u*, **in those roots**

e. g. piluv (u) + a lēd = piluvalēdu పిలువలేదు

čhood (u) + ,, = čhoodalēdu చూడలేదు

etc. etc

Note the following past negative forms carefully :—

kālēdu కాలేదు —did not become.

ceyalēdu చేయలేదు—did not give.

thēlēdu తేలేదు —did not get.

pōlēdu పోలేదు —did not go.

lēvalēdu లేవలేదు —did not rise.

Now read the following negative sentences in the future tense :—

nēnu chēy*anu*	నేను చేయను	—*I shall not* do.
mēmu chēy*amu*	మేము చేయము	—*we shall not* do.
neevu chēy*avu*	నీవు చేయవు	—*you* (thou) *will not* do.
meeru chēy*aru*	మీరు చేయరు	—*you will not* do.
vādu chēy*adu*	వాడు చేయడు	—*he will not* do.
āme chēy*ad̄u*	ఆమె చేయదు	—*she will not* do.
ad̄i chēy*ad̄u*	అది చేయదు	—*it will not* do.
vāru chēy*aru*	వారు చేయరు	—*they will not* do.
avi chēy*avu*	అవి చేయవు	— ,,
nēnu c̄hood*anu*	నేను చూడను	—*I shall not* see.
mēmu rā*mu*	మేము రాము	—*we shall not* come
vāru thē*ru*	వారు తేరు	—*they will not* get.
meeru pō*ru*	మీరు పోరు	—*you will not* go.

From the above santences it will be seen that **the negative in the future tense is formed by adding the following terminations to the "changed roots" (colloquial imperative mood), after removing the last *u* thereof**, in the same way as the past tense negative terminations are added.

Person	**Singular**	**Plural**
1st	anu అను	amu అము
2nd	avu అవు	aru అరు
3rd	adu అడు (for a male)	aru అరు (for human beings)
	ad̄u అదు (for others)	avu అవు (for others)

e. g. C̄hood (u) + anu—choodanu చూడను
= (I) will not see.

piluvu (u) + aru—piluvaru పిలువరు
you (they) will not call.

Note the following future negative formations carefully :—

"Changed Root"	**Formations**
kā కా	kānu కాను, kāmu కాము. kādu కాదు etc.
eeyu ఈయు	eeyanu ఈయను, eeyadu ఈయడు etc.
pō పో	pōnu పోను pōru పోరు pōdu పోడు etc.
rā రా	rānu రాను, rāmu రాము etc.
lēvu లేవు	lēvanu లేవను, lēvadu లేవడు etc.
thē తే	thēnu తేను, thēru తేరు etc.

Now, read the following negative verbs in the **Imperative mood :—**

piluva*kumu* పిలువకుము—Do not call.
C̄hooda*kumu* చూడకుము—Do not see.
chē*yakumu* చేయకుము—Do not do.
thina*kumu* తినకుము—Don't eat.
thē*kumu* తేకుము— Don't get.

These and other negative verbs in the Imperative mood are formed by adding *akumu* అకుము in the singular and *akudu* అకుడు in the plural to the "changed root" (in the same way as negative terminations for the past and the future tenses are added. Note carefully the following negative verbs in the imperative mood :—

"Changed Root"	**Negative-Imperative -Singular**	**Plural**
kā కా	k*ā kumu* *కాకుము* (Don't became)	kākudu కాకుడు.
eeyu ఈయు	eeya*kumu* ఈయకుము (Don't give)	eeyakudu ఈయకుడు.
pō పో	pō*kumu* పోకుము (Don't go)	pōkudu పోకుడు.
rā రా	rākumu రాకుము (Don't come)	rākudu రాకుడు
lēvu లేవు	lēvakumu లేవకుము (Don't rise)	lēvakudu లేవకుడు.
thē తే	thēkumu తేకుము (Don't get)	thēkudu తేకుడు.

The termination *avad̄d̄u* అవద్దు (or *avalad̄u* అవలదు) also **is generally used** to form the negative in the imperative mood. This termination should be added to the "changed root" in the same way as other terminations are added.

See the following examples :—

chood*avad̄d̄u* చూడవద్దు—don't see.
chē*yavad̄d̄u* చేయవద్దు—don't do.
pō*vad̄d̄u* పోవద్దు—don't go.
ra*vad̄d̄u* రావద్దు—don't come.
eey*avad̄d̄u* ఈయవద్దు—don't give.

---

* This last *mu* ము may be omitted in speakink to a child, servant etc.

thē*vaddu* తేవద్దు —don't get.
C̄hāva*vad̄d̄u* చావవద్దు —don't die.
kott*avad̄d̄u* కొట్టవద్దు —don't beat.
thitt*avad̄d̄u* తిట్టవద్దు —don't blame.

meeru kriketu pandemulu C̄hoochithira ? మీరు క్రికెటు పందెములు చూచితిరా ?—did you see cricket matches ?

lēd̄u, nēnu C̄hoodalēd̄u లేదు, నేను చూడలేదు—No, I did not see.

ayithē nēdu vathurā ? అయితే నేడు వత్తురా ?—if so, will (you) come today ?

lēd̄u, nēnu nēdu rānu లేదు నేను నేడు రాను—no, I will not come today.

end̄uku ఎందుకు ?—way ?

nēnu nēdu vērē pani meed̄a pōvuchunnānu నేను నేడు వేరే పనిమీద పోవుచున్నాను—today I am going on another business.

mee thammudu vaC̄hchunā ? మీ తమ్ముడు వచ్చునా?—will your brother come ?

lēd̄u, nā thammudu kooda rādu లేదు, నా తమ్ముడు కూడ రాడు—no, my brother also will not come.

athadu oorilō lēdu అతడు ఊరిలో లేడు—He is not in the station.

ayithē mee kumārudu āta sthalamunaku vaC̄hchuna ? అయితే మీ కుమారుడు ఆటస్థలమునకు వచ్చునా ?— If so, will your son come to the play-ground ?

ounu, athadu vaC̄hchunu ఔను, అతడు వచ్చును—yes, he will come.

kāni konchemu ālasyamu agunu కాని కొంచెము ఆలస్యము అగును --But (there) will be some delay.

meeru undavad̄d̄u మీరు ఉండవద్దు—Don't wait.

nāyanā! nēnu kood̄a pōvud̄unu నాయనా! నేను కూడ పోవుదును Father! I will also go.

vad̄d̄u, neevu ippudu pōvad̄d̄u వద్దు, నీవు ఇప్పుడు పోవద్దు—No, Don't go now.

neevu nee pātthamulu C̄had̄uva vad̄d̄a ? నీవు నీ పాఠములు చేదువ వద్దా ?—Don't you have to read your lessons ?

nenu ippudu pātthamulu C̄had̄uvanu నేను ఇప్పుడు పాఠములు చేదువను—I don't read (my) lessons now.

nenu rēpu C̄had̄uvud̄unu నేను రేపు చదువుదును—I will read (my lessons) tomorrow.

manchid̄i, ayithe neevu kooda pō మంచిది, అయితే నీవుకూడ పో—well, if it is so, you also go.

godugu theesikoni pōvuC̄hunnāyā ? గొడుగు తీసికొని పోవుచున్నావా ?—Are you taking (away the) umbrella ?

lēd̄u, nēnu godugu theesikoni pōvutalēd̄u లేదు నేను గొడుగు తీసికొని పోవుటలేదు—No, I am not taking (away the) umbrella.

meeru ālasyamu chēyakudu మీరు ఆలస్యము చేయకుడు—Don't delay.

LESSON 8

Grammar

Pronouns

Pronouns are used in the place of nouns to avoid unnecessary repetition of the latter. The principal pronouns are given below. Instructions as to the application of case terminations (prepositions) to pronouns are also given below.

PRONOUNS WITH ENGLISH MEANING	POSSESSIVE CASE
vādu వాడు —he athadu అతడు—he (that man or boy)	vāni వాని athani అతని } —his
veedu వీడు ithadu ఇతడు } —this man or boy	veeni వీని ithani ఇతని } —this man's (or) boy's
evadu ఎవడు —who (for a male only)	evani ఎవని —whose
vāru వారు—they (human beings only)	vāri వారి —their
veeru వీరు —these people	veeri వీరి —of these people
evaru ఎవరు—who (plural human beings)	evari ఎవరి —whose
thāmu తాము thamaru తమరు } —you	thamari తమరి —your
adi అది —it, that	dāni దాని —its, of that
idi ఇది —this	deeni దీని —of this
ēdi ఏది —what, which (singular)	dēni దేని —of what

avi అవి—they, those (other than human beings	vāni వాని—their
ivi ఇవి—these ,,	veeni వీని—of these
ēvi ఏవి—what, which(plural)	vēni వేని—of what

The possessive * case forms given on the right above are very important as they help in forming other cases.

Objective case of the above pronouns is fromed by adding *ni* ని to the possessive case form.

e. g.
vāni*ni* వానిని } —him
athani*ni* అతనిని }
vāri*ni* వారిని —them
evani*ni* ఎవనిని (singular) } —whom
evari*ni* ఎవరిని (plural) }

Adding *ki* కి to the possessive case forms of the above pronouns gives the meaning of the English preposition "to".

e. g.
vāni +ki = vāniki వానికి—to him
vāri +ki = vāriki వారికి—to them
evani +ki = evaniki ఎవనికి } —to whom
evari +ki = evariki ఎవరికి }
dāni +ki = dāniki దానికి—to it.

Now, set the following pronouns and their possessive case forms :—

---

* *yokka* యొక్క (—of) may or may not be added to these forms; it is all the same.

PRONOUN	POSSESSIVE ("of")	OBJECTIVE CASE
neevu నీవు—you (thou)	nee నీ—your	ninnu నిన్ను—you
meeru మీరు—you	mee మీ—your	mimmu మిమ్ము-you
nēnu నేను—I	nā నా—my	nannu నన్ను—me
mēmu మేము—we (he/they & I)	mā మా—our	mammu మమ్ము-us
thānu తాను—he / she	thana తన—his / her	thananu తనను-him / her
thāmu తాము-they	thama తమ—their	thamanu తమను—them
manamu మనము—we (you & I)	mana మన—our	mananu మనను—us
āme ఆమె—she	āme ఆమె—her	ā menu ఆమెను -her

For getting the meaning of the English preposition "To" along with the above eight pronouns, add *ku* కు to the possessive case form.

e. g. mana + ku = manaku మనకు—to us (to me & to you)

mā + ku = māku మాకు — to us (to me & him/them)

nee + ku = neeku నీకు —to you (singular)

mee + ku = meeku మీకు —to you (plural)

nā + ku = nāku నాకు —to me.

The preposition *goorchi* గూర్చి (gurinchi గురించి) meaning "about", is added to the objective case forms of all the pronouns.

e. g. vānini +goorchi వానిని గూర్చి —about him
āmenu +gurinchi ఆమెను గురించి —about her
nannu +goorchi నన్ను గూర్చి —about me
ninnu +goorchi నిన్ను గూర్చి —about you.

All other prepositions (case terminations) are to be added to the possessive case forms of the pronouns.

e. g. nā +thō నాతో —with me
mee +venta మీ వెంట —along with you
vāni +vīpu వాని వైపు —towards him
mā +koraku మాకొఱకు —for us
āme +chētha ఆమె చేత —by her
vāri +nundi వారి నుండి —from them
dēni +lō దేని లో —in which
evari +meeda ఎవరి మీద —on whom

Read the following sentences :—

ā balla nādi ఆ బల్ల నాది—that bench *is mine*.

ee kurchee meedi ఈ కుర్చీ మీది—this chair *is yours*.

ā kalamu vānidi ఆ కలము వానిది—that pen *is his*.

ee pusthakamu evaridi ఈ పుస్తకము ఎవరిది ?—*Whose* book is this ?—

ee indlu nā*vi* ఈ ఇండ్లు నావి—these houses *are mine*.

ā battalu vāri*vi* ఆ బట్టలు వారివి—those cloths *are theirs*.

ee pencillu āmevi ఈ పెన్సిల్లు ఆమెవి—these pencils *are hers*.

ā pusthakamulu evarivi ఆ పుస్తకములు ఎవరివి?—**whose books** *are those ?*

From the above sentences you will see **that the** addition of di ది (for singular) **and** *vi* వి **(for plural) to** pronouns in the possessive case gives **us the double** possessive.

EXERCISE

upayōgakaramagu	ఉపయోగకరమగు	—usefull
kāvali kāyu	కావలి కాయు	—to keep watch
thōka	తోక	—tail
visvāsamugala	విశ్వాసముగల	—faithful
māmsamu	మాంసము	—meat
kathha	కథ	—story.

Kukka కుక్క — The Dog.

kukka chāla upayōgakaramagu janthuvu కుక్క చాల ఉపయోగకరమగు జంతువు—The dog (is) (a) very useful animal.

adi mana indlaku kāvali kāyunu అది మన ఇండ్లకు కావలి కాయును—It keeps watch over our houses.

kukka vadigā parugeththunu కుక్క వడిగా పరుగెత్తును—(The) dog runs fast.

kukkaku nālugu kāllu unnavi కుక్కకు నాలుగు కాళ్లు ఉన్నవి
—(A) dog has four legs.
—(There) are four legs to (the) dog.

dāniki oka thōka unnadi దానికి ఒక తోక ఉన్నది—**It has a tail.**

kukkalalō chāla rakamulu kalavu కుక్కలలో చాలరకములు కలవు—(There) are many kinds of dogs.

kukka viswāsamugala janthuvu కుక్క విశ్వాసముగల జంతువు—(The) dog (is) (a) faithful animal.

adi gaddi thinadu అది గడ్డి తినదు—It does not eat grass.

adi annamu, māmsamu thinunu అది అన్నము, మాంసము తినును It eats food (and) meat.

kukkalanu gurinchi chāla kathhalu kalavu కుక్కలను గురించి చాల కథలు కలవు—(There) are many stories about dogs.

LESSON 9

Adjective

Some adjectives which are generally used in daily routine are given in the ' vocabulary" section of this book. The following table shows how to use terminations to forms adjectives :—

Termination	To be added to	Meaning.	Examples.
ina ఇన	root	Past participle—adjective.	Chooch*ina* చూచిన—which was, or has been seen. vin*ina* వినిన—which was, or has been heard. nēnu thin*ina* pandu నేను తినిన పండు—the fruit eaten by me.
ani అని; anatti అనట్టి	changed root	negative adjective	thin*ani* తినని—not eaten. vin*ani* వినని—not heard. Chood*anatti* చూడనట్టి—not seen. kōr*anatti* కోరనట్టి—not desired.

C̄hunna చున్న	root	present participle	kaḏalu*chunna* కదలుచున్న—moving vaC̄hchu*chunna* sthree వచ్చుచున్న స్త్రీ-comming woman. Povu*chunna* manushyudu పోవుచున్న మనుష్యుడు—going man.
edi ఎడి ; edu ఎడు	root	adjective present or, future tense	po*yedi* పోయెడి—who/which will go; or who/which is going. — or vaC̄hch*edu* వచ్చెడు—who/which will come; or, who/which is coming. — or
agala అగల	changed root	able to (do) (adjective)	ād*agala* ఆడగల—able to play pād*agala* పాడగల—able to sing chood*agala* చూడగల—able to see
alēni అలేని	changed root	unable to do	vin*aleni* వినలేని—unable to hear r*aleni* రాలేని—unable to come polēni పోలేని—unable to go C̄hoodalēni చూడలేని—unable to see.

arāni అరాని akoodani అకూడని	changed root	which should not be (done)	thin*arāni* తినరాని **or** thinakoodani తినకూడని —which should not be eaten. vin*arāni* వినరాని vinakoodani వినకూడని — which should not be heard,
gala గల unna ఉన్న unna ఉన్న	**noun** **noun** **adverb**	having having being	illu*gala* ఇల్లుగల—having (a) house illu*nna* ఇల్లు ఉన్న—having (a) house sukhamugā *unna* సుఖముగా ఉన్న— (being) happy.
lēni లేని	noun or adverb	not having or not being.	nōru *lēni* నోరులేని—having no voice, *ie* who is unable to bawl out; (innocent) vēdigā*lēni* వేడిగాలేని—not hot.
inantha ఇనంత	root	as much as	chēs*inantha* చేసినంత—as much as is (or was) done. Chooch*inantha* చూచినంత—as much as is (or was) seen.
inanni ఇనన్ని	root	as many as	thin*inanni* తినినన్ని—as many as are eaten. kor*inanni* కోరినన్ని—as many as desired.

When a noun or a pronoun is used as a complement to a predicate, *ie* to complete the sense (meaning of a verb), the following terminations are added to such a noun or pronoun :—

PERSON	If the noun ends in *i* ఇ		if the noun enns in a letter other than *i* ఇ	
	SINGULAR	PLURAL	SINGULAR	PLURAL
1st	ni ని	amu అము	anu అను	amu అము
2nd	vi వి	(arm అరు	avu అవు	(aru అరు)
3rd	—	—	—	—

(terminations in brackets may or may not be used.)

e. g. nēnu Har*ini* నేను హరిని —I (am) Hari

neevu rō*givi* నీవు రోగివి—you (are) a patient.

memu kavu*lamu* మేము కవులము—we are poets.

meeru manchivaru or manchivaralu మీరు మంచివారు (మంచివారలు)

nēnu manchivādanu నేను మంచివాడను.

when pronouns are qualified by adjectives, the following affirmative and negative terminations are added :-

Affirmative.

PERSON & SEX	SINGULAR.	PLURAL.
1st (male)	vādanu వాడను	varāmu వారము
(female)	dānanu దానను	
2nd (male)	vādavu వాడవు	vāru వారు
(female)	dānavu దానవు	
3rd (male)	vādu వాడు	vāru వారు (fo human beings)
(others) di ది		vi వి (for others)

NEGATIVE

1st	gānu గాను	gāmu గాము
2nd	gāvu గావు	gāru గారు
3rd (male)	gādu గాడు	gāru గారు (for human beings)
(others)	gād̄u గాదు	gāvu గావు (others).

See the following examples.

nēnu manchi vādanu నేను మంచి వాడను
—I am a good man

nĕnu ped̄d̄ad̄ānanu నేను పెద్దదానను
—I am an elderly woman

neevu chedda vādavu gāvu నీవు చెడ్డవాడవు గావు
—you are not a bad man

neevu chinnad̄ānavu gāvu నీవు చిన్నదానవు గావు
—you are not an young woman

ā koora manchid̄i gād̄u ఆ కూర మంచిది గాదు
—that vegetable is not good.

LESSON 10

Verbs

You have already learnt the termination for the past, present and future tenses. There are alternative sets of terminations for the past and future tenses. They are given below. These alternative terminations also are in common use and are applied to roots in the same way as the first set are used. It is better to revise the lessons on Past & Future Tenses before taking up this lesson.

Future Tense

PERSON.	SINGULAR.	PLURAL.
1st	ed̄anu ఎదను	ed̄amu ఎదము
2nd	ed̄avu ఎదవు	ed̄aru ఎదరు
3rd	nu ను	ed̄aru ఎదరు (for human beings) nu ను (for others.)

e. g. Čhad̄ived̄anu చదివెదను—I will read
chēsed̄aru చేసెదరు —you/they will do.
thined̄amu తినెదము —we shall eat.
ād̄ed̄avu ఆడెదవు —you will play.

This set of termination also is used to tell about events which are natural and or which occur usually.

Paste Tense.

PERSON	SINGULAR.	PLURAL.
1st	inānu ఇనాను	in$^{\bar{a}}$mu ఇనాము
2nd	in$^{\bar{a}}$vu ఇనావు	in$^{\bar{a}}$ru ఇనారు
3rd	in$^{\bar{a}}$du ఇనాడు (for a male)	ināru ఇనారు (for human beings)
	inadi ఇనది (for others)	inavi ఇనవి (for others.)

e. g. Chadiv*inānu* చదివినాను—I read (or I have read)

chēsin*ādu* చేసినాడు —He did (or has done)

Choochi*nāru* చూచినారు—you/they saw (or have seen)

thinin*āvu* తినినావు—you ate (or have eaten)

Note that this set of terminations is used for the present perfect tense also as shown above. Some more examples are given below :—

nēnu ippudē vachchin$^{\bar{a}}$nu నేను ఇప్పుడే వచ్చినాను—I *have* come just now.

v$^{\bar{a}}$ru kooda ippudē vachchin^{a}ru వారు కూడ ఇప్పుడే వచ్చినారు—They also *have come* just now.

āme p$^{\bar{a}}$tthamulu Chadivinadi ఆమె పాఠములు చదివినది—She *has read* (her) lessons (now).

The present participle.

vādu *pādu*chu koorčhundenu వాడు పాడుచు కూర్చుండెను—He sat sing*ing*.

mēmu *māṭalādu*chu pōyithimi మేము మాటలాడుచు పోయితిమి —We went talk*ing*.

In the above sentences the words in italics ara present participles. They mean incomplete action at e particular time. They are formed by adding *čhu* చు to the roots.

e. g. vačhchu + čhu—వచ్చుచు
pōvu + čhu—పోవుచు
thinu + čhu—తినుచు
chēyu + čhu—చేయుచు

The past participle.

nēnu *pōyi* čhoochithini నేను పోయి చూచితిని—Having gone, I saw (—I went and saw.)

vādu *vachchi* thinenu వాడు వచ్చి తినెను—Having come, he ate (—He came and ete.)

In the above sentences, the words in italics tell about the first action which had been completed before the second one began. These are past participles. They are formed by adding *i* ఇ to the root (after removing the last *u* thereof) e. g.

thin*i* తిని —having eaten.
thrāg*i* త్రాగి —having drunk.
chē*si* చేసి —having done.
kō*si* కోసి —having cut.

The present perfect Tense :— We have already told about one method to form this tense. Now we give another method which is to add the present tense formations of the root *undu* ఉండు to the past participle of the principal verb.

e. g. thini + unnādu తిని యున్నాడు
—he has eaten. (—తినినాడు)

chēsi + unnādu చేసి యున్నాడు
—he has done. (—చేసినాడు)

vini + unnādu విని యున్నాడు
—he has heard. (—వినినాడు)

Here note that the vowel *u* ఉ coming immediately after a past participle is changed to యు *yu*.

The past perfect tense :—

nēnu pōvunappatiki vādu *vachchi yundenu* నేను పోవునప్పటికి వాడు వచ్చియుండెను—he *had come* before I went.

neevu vachchunappatiki nēnu *pōyiyuntini* నీవు వచ్చునప్పటికి నేను పోయియుంటిని—I *had gone* before you came.

The words in italics in the above sentences are in the past perfect tense, which is formed by adding the past tense termination of the root *undu* ఉండు to the past participle of the principle verb.

The past continuous tense.

kukkalu *moruguchundenu* కుక్కలు మొఱుగుచుండెను—Dogs *were barking.*

manushyulu *parugeththuchundiri* మనుష్యులు పరుగెత్తుచుండిరి —Men *were running.*

These words in italics are in the Past continuous tense which is formed by adding the past tense form of the root *undu* to the present participle of the principal verb.

This formation denotes a past habit also.

e. g. vāru tharachu mā intiki vachchuchundiri వారు తఱచు మా ఇంటికి వచ్చుచుండిరి—They *used to come* to our house often.

The Future continuous tense:

nēnu rēpatinundi mee yoddaku *vachchuchundunu* నేను రేపటినుండి మీ యొద్దకు వచ్చుచుందును—I *shall be coming* to you from tomorrow.

This tense is formed by adding the future tense formation of the root *undu* ఉండు to the present participle of the principal verb (Here note that the *u* ఉ of the root undu ఉండు is dropped while adding to the present participle).

CAN & CANNOT

chē*yagalanu* చేయగలను—I can do

,, mu ,, ము—we ,,

,, vu ,, వు—you ,,

,, ru ,, రు—you ,,

,, du ,, డు—he ,,

,, d̄u ,, దు—{she / it} ,,

,, ru ,, రు—they ,, (human beings)

,, vu ,, వు— ,, ,, (others.)

chē*yalenu* చేయలేను—I cannot do

,, mu ,, ము—we cannot do

chēyalevu చేయలేవు—you (thou) cannot do

,, ru ,, రు—you cannot do

,, du ,, డు—he cannot do

,, d̄u ,, దు—she/it cannot do

,, ru ,, రు—they (human beings) cannot do

,, vu ,, వు— ,, (others) cannot do.

From the above examples it will be seen that the Telugu terminations for "can" and "cannot" are as follows :—

Person	Can		Cannot	
	SINGULAR	PLURAL	SINGULAR	PLURAL
1st	agalanu అగలను	agalamu అగలము	alēnu అలేను	alēmu అలేము
2nd	agalavu అగలవు	agalaru అగలరు	alēvu అలేవు	alēru అలేరు
3rd	agaladu అగలడు (for male)	agalaru అగలరు (fot human beings)	alēdu అలేడు (for male)	alēru అలేరు (for human beings)
,,	agaladu అగలదు (for others)	agalavu అగలవు (for others)	alēdu అలేదు (for others)	alēvu అలేవు (for others)

These terminations are to be added to the "*changed roots*" (colloquial Imperative mood).

e. g. rā + (a) galanu రాగలను—I can come.
rā + (a) lēdu రాలేడు —He cannot come.
Chood (u) + agalamu చూడగలము—we can see.
cey (u) + alēru ఇయ్యలేరు—you/they cannot give.

In the above negative terminations, (for "cannot") the letters *alē* అలే can be replaced by the letters *ajāla* అజాల. Both mean the same thing.

e. g. r*ālē*du రాలేడు — r*ājāla*du రాజాలడు — He cannot come.

ch*ē*y*alē*mu చేయలేము — chēya*jala*mu చేయజాలము— we cannot do.

The terminations given in the following list are very useful in getting many necessary verbal formations. Almost all the terminations beginning with the vowel *a* అ should be added to the "changed root" (same as the colloquial imperative mood form) and almost all others should be added to the original roots. A few original roots with the relative "changed roots" are shown below for the student's ready reference :—

original roots		**"changed roots"**	
vaC̄hchu	వచ్చు	rä	రా
thinu	తిను	thinu	తిను
C̄hooC̄hu	చూచు	C̄hoodu	చూడు
pŌvu	పోవు	pŌ	పో
theC̄hchu	తెచ్చు	thē	తే
grahimC̄hu	గ్రహించు	grahimpu	గ్రహింపు
lēchu	లేచు	lēvu	లేవు

Termination	to be added to	Meaning	Examples
i ఇ	root	Past participle (continuative) having (done)	Čhoočhi చూచి—having seen thini తిని—having eaten vachchi వచ్చి—having come chēsi చేసి—having done pōyi పోయి—having gone koni కొని—having bought
aka అక or akunda అకుండ	changed root	negative—not having (done) = without (doing)	Čhoodaka చూడక—not having seen thinaka తినక—not having eaten rāka రాక—not having come chēyaka చేయక—not having done pōka పోక—not having gone konaka కొనక—not having bought ammakunda అమ్మకుండ-not having sold levakunda లేవకుండ—not having risen or without rising.

C̄hu చే	root	Present participle (do) ing	vinuC̄hu వినుచే—hearing kaD̄aluC̄hu కదలుచే—moving C̄hooC̄huC̄hu చూచేచే — seeing (he went seeing) pāduC̄hu పాడుచే—singing (he stood singing)
C̄hundaka చేండక	root	(negative) not (do) ing—without (do) ing.	vrāyuC̄hundaka—వ్రాయుచేండక without writing (not writing) C̄haD̄uvuC̄hundaka చదువుచేండక —without reading.
akundu అకుండు	changed root	negative of the root —not to (do)	vinakundu వినకుండు—not to hear thinakundu తినకుండు—not to eat C̄hoodakundu చూడకుండు—not to see

ta ట	root	gerund—(do) ing	thinuta తినుట—eating vinuta వినుట—hearing chepputa చెప్పుట—saying chēyuta చేయుట—doing (*saying* is different from *doing*)
akunduta అకుండుట or ami అమి	changed root	negative of the gerund —not (do) ing	thinakunduta తినకుండుట—not eating vinami వినమి—or vinakunduta వినకుండుట—not hearing (*Not hearing* my words is no good)
C̄hunda చుండ or C̄hundagā చుండగా	root	while (do) ing	pŌvuC̄hunda (gā) పోవుచుండ (గా) —while going vaC̄hchuC̄hunda (gā) వచ్చుచుండ (గా) —while coming chēyuC̄hunda (gā) చేయుచుండ (గా) —while doing.

avalenu అవలెను or nad̄i నది	changed root	should (do) —command and	thēvalenu తేవలెను—should get pōvalenu పోవలెను—should go. c̄hoodavalenu చూడవలెను—should see
	root		thinunad̄i తినునది—should eat vac̄hchunad̄i వచ్చునది—should come vrāyunad̄i వ్రాయునది—should write c̄had̄uvavalenu చదువవలెను—should read
arād̄u అరాదు or akoodad̄u అకూడదు	changed root	should not (do)—command *or* advice.	kad̄alakoodad̄u కదలకూడదు—should not move vinarād̄u వినరాదు—should not hear pōrād̄u పోరాదు—or pōkoodad̄u పోకూడదు—should not go
iyundakoodad̄u యుండకూడదు	root	should not have (done)—prohibition, past tense	thiniyunda koodad̄u తినియుండ కూడదు —should not have eaten pōyiyundakoodad̄u పోయియుండకూడదు —should not have (gone)

C̄hunda-koodad̄u చుండకూడదు	root	should not be (do)ing —prohibition —present tense	nadaC̄huC̄hunda koodad̄u నడచుచుండ కూడదు—should not be walking vinuC̄hunda koodad̄u వినుచుండకూడదు —should not be hearing.
avaC̄hchunu అవచ్చును	changed root	may—permission. possibility, or, probability	kona vaC̄hchunu కొనవచ్చును—may buy kāvaC̄hchunu కావచ్చును—may be, or, may become. pŌvaC̄hchunu పోవచ్చును—may go rāvaC̄hchunu రావచ్చును—may come
akapŌvaC̄hchunu అకపోవచ్చును	changed root	may not (do) Improbability—present, or, future.	C̄hoodaka pŌvaC̄hchunu చూడక పోవచ్చును—may not see. rākapŌvaC̄hchunu రాకపోవచ్చును—may not come. thinaka pŌvaC̄hchunu తినకపోవచ్చును —may not eat.

iyunda vaC̄hchunu ఇయుండవచ్చును	root	might have (done)—permission, possibility, or, probability—past tense	vaC̄hchiyundavaC̄hchunu వచ్చియుండ వచ్చును—might have come C̄hoochiynnda vaC̄hchunu చూచియుండ వచ్చును—might have seen. pilichiyundavaC̄hchunu పిలిచియుండ వచ్చును—might have called.
iyundaka pŌvaC̄hchunu ఇయుండక పోవచ్చును	root	might not have (done)—Improbability past tense.	anD̄iyundakapŌvaC̄hchunu అందియుండక పోవచ్చును—might not have reached. C̄hoochiyundaka pŌvaC̄hchnun చూచియుండక పోవచ్చును—might not have seen.
agaligi yunda vaC̄hchunu అగలిగి యుండ వచ్చును	changed root	might be, *or* might have been, able to (do)—. doubt as to the ability to (do)— three tenses.	cheppagaligi yundavaC̄hchunu చెప్పగలిగి యుండవచ్చును—might be, *or* might have been able to tell, C̄hoodagaligi yundavaC̄hchunu చూడగలిగి యుండ వచ్చును—might be, or, might have been, able to see.

ajālakunda vaČhchunu అజాలకుండవచ్చును	changed root	might not be, *or* might not have been able to (do)--doubt as to the inability to do—three tenses	konajālakundavaČhchunu కొనజాలకుండ వచ్చును—might not be, or, might not have been, able to buy.
avalasiyundunu అవలసియుండును	changed root	will have to (do)—duty—future tense	cheppavalasiyundunu చెప్పవలసియుం డును—will have to tell. Čhoodavalasiyundunu చూడవలసి యుండును—will have to see.
avalasi yunde nu అవలసియుండెను	changed root	ought to have (done —a thing which) was to be done but was not actually done.	rāvalasiyundenu రావలసియుండెను— ought to have come (but did not come). Pōvalasiyundenu పోవలసియుండెను— ought to have gone (but did not go.)
avalasivachche-nu అవలసివచ్చెను	changed root	had to (do)—Čom-pulsion—past tense	Čhampavalasivachchenu చంపవలసివచ్చెను —had to kill.

Chunda vaChchunu చుండవచ్చును	root	may be, or, might have been, (doing) permission, or probability continuous.	vinuChundavaChchunu వినుచుండవచ్చును may be, or might have been, hearing.
inchu *ఇంచు	root	causative	chēyinchu చేయించు—to get (it) done (by somebody else). vrāyinchu వ్రాయించు—to get (it) written (by somebody else). koyinChu కోయించు—to get (it) cut (by some body else).

*When this termination is added, many roots change their forms materially. As it is not possible to show all those changes here, the student is instructed to observe them while reading Telugu books. Generally, causative forms may be obtained by adding the termination "ajēyu అజేయు" to the "changed root" as already explained in the previous pages.

abadu అబడు	changed root	passive voice *	C̄hoodabadu చూడబడు—to be seen vrāyabadu వ్రాయబడు—to be written mōyabadu మోయబడు—to be carried thinabadenu తినబడెను—was eaten padavēyabadiri పడవేయబడిరి—were thrown (down) cheppabadinadi చెప్పబడినది—has been told chēyabaduchunnadi చేయబడుచున్నది—is being done lāgabadunu లాగబడును—will be pulled
C̄hō చో	root	"if" **or** "when"—future tense only	pōvuchō పోవుచో—if, or, when (I, he, etc) will go,— thinuC̄hō తినుచో—if, or, when (I, he they, etc) will eat.

* In Telugu passive voice is very rarely used- Therefore, no special treatment has been given to this heading in this book.

ina ఇన; inac̄hō ఇనచో or inayedala ఇనయెడల	root	"if"—all tenses'	vachina (c̄hō) వచ్చిన (చో) or vachinayedala వచ్చినయెడల–if (I, they, etc) come or came...... pōyina (c̄hō) పోయిన (చో) or pōyinayedala పోయినయెడల-if (I, they, etc) go or went.
ēni ఏని	future or past tense forms of verbs.	"if"—future or past tenses.	vaththurēni వత్తురేని–if (they) come... vachirēni వచ్చిరేని—if (they) came
anic̄hō అనిచో or aniyedala అనియెడల	changed root	if......not	naduvanic̄hō నడువనిచో or naduvaniyedala నడువనియెడల—if (you etc) do *not* walk. rānic̄hō రానిచో or rāniyedala రానియెడల—if (you etc) do not come pōnic̄hō పోనిచో or pōniyedala పోనియెడల—if (you etc) do not go.

iyundinacho ఇయుండినచో or iyundina yedala ఇయుండిన యెడల	root	had (I etc) (done)—unfulfilled conditional-affirmative	vaC̄hchiyundinaC̄ho వచ్చియుండినచో or vaC̄hchiyundinayedala వచ్చియుండిన యెడల —(they etc) come, (*i. e*, If they came, something would have happended. They did not come and something did not happen).
iyundaniC̄hŌ ఇయుండనిచో or iyundani yedala ఇయుండని యెడల	root	had (you etc) not (done so)—unfulfilled condition negative.	vaC̄hchiyundaniC̄ho వచ్చియుండనిచో *or* vaC̄hchiyundaniyedala వచ్చియుండని యెడల—had (you) not come, (something would have happened). (because you came, something did not happen).
napudu నపుడు *or* nappudu నప్పుడు	root	when (do) ing	pŌvunapudu పోవునపుడు—when going vaC̄hchunappudu వచ్చునప్పుడు — when coming.
ēmŌ ఏమో or Ō lēdŌ ఓ లేదో	a verb in any of the three tenses	whether (or) not...	pŌyenēmŌ పోయెనేమో— whether (he) weut (or not) vaC̄hchenŌlēdŌ వచ్చెనో,లేదో—whether (he) came or not

animmu అనిమ్ము (1) **or** anidu అనిండు (2)	changed root	let, (us, him etc) (do)	choodanimmu చూడనిమ్ము— **or** choodanindu చూడనిండు — let (us, him, them, etc) see. (1) is addressed to one person (2) is addressed to tWo or more persons.
lemmu లెమ్ము (1) **or** lendu లెండు (2)	a verb in any tense	(that is alright, don't worry.	pŌvunu lemmu పోవును లెమ్ము— (that is alright) it will go, (don't worry) (1) is addressed to one person (2) is addressed to one or more persons.
gāka గాక ! **or** gātha గాత !	root or a verb in a future tense	may......... (benediction.)	chēyugāka చేయుగాక — may (he etc) do. īChugātha ఇచ్చుగాత — may (he etc) give.
a, aga అ అగ. agā అగా	changed root	for (do) ing; on (do) ing	vina bōyenu వినబోయెను —went for hearing. vinaga వినగ for hearing Choodagā చూడగా.for seeing;on seeing

Compound Verbs :

In English, Various prepositions are added to the verbs to give different meanings.

e. g. to go out — to go on
to go away — to go in for, etc.

In Telugu, one root is joined to another root to give a different shade of meaning. These are called compound verbs.

e. g. ṇērchu + konu నేర్చుకొను—to learn.

Generally, the principal root (the first one) changes its form when the second root is added. But all the terminations for tenses etc, are added to the second root only. Some roots which help to form compound verbs are given below :—

Second root	To which form of the principal verbs added.	Meaning.	Examples.
konu కొను	added to the Past Participle of transitive verbs ending in	(doing for one's own use and not for others.)	(1) vandikonu వండికొను **or** vandukonu వండుకొను—to cook for one-self.

Second root	To which form of the principal verbs added	Meaning.	Examples.
	yu యు and to the roots or Past participles of other transitive verbs.		(2) vrāsikonu వ్రాసికొను—to write for one-self. (3) chaduvukonu చదువుకొను **or** chadivikonu చదివికొను— to read for one's self.
abōvu అబోవు (from the root pōvu పోవు)	"changed root"	(about to do.)	(1) thinabōvu తినబోవు—about to eat (2) Choodabōvu చూడబోవు-about to see (3) mringabōyenu మ్రింగబోయెను—(He) was about to swallow.
vēyu వేయు	Past participles of transitive verbs. "changed root" of transitive verbs.	Express force, and completion (like the English preposition "of"	(1) kōsivēyu కోసివేయు—to cut off. (2) padavēyu పడవేయు–to throw down

Second root	To which form of the principal verbs added	Meaning.	Examples
alēkapōvu అలేకపోవు (from the root) pōvu పోవు	"changed root"	to be unable to do	(1) Chood*alekapōyithini* చూడలేకపోయితిని (I) was unable to see. (I could not see). (2) ammalēkapōvunu అమ్మలేకపోవును— (He) will not be able to sell. (3) thinalēka pōvuchunnādu తినలేక పోవుచున్నాడు —He is unable to eat.
anichchu అనిచ్చు (from the root ichchu ఇచ్చు).	changed root	to allow, to let one to do something	(1) Choodanichu చూడనిచ్చు—to allow one to see. (2) pōnichchu పోనిచ్చు—to let one go. (3) pōnimmu—let......go.
asāgu అసాగు or aḍodagu అడొడగు	do.	to begin to do something (from the roots sāgu & thodagu	(1) chēyasāgu చేయసాగు—to begin to do. (2) Choodaḍodagu చూడదొడగు— to begin to see.
agōru అగోరు (from the root kōru కోరు)	changed root	to desire to do something	Choodagōru చూడగోరు—to desire to see.

Second root	To which form of the principal verbs added.	Meaning.	Examples.
theeru తీరు	Past Participle	to do something without fail	vachitheeru వచ్చితీరు—to come without fail.
ajēyu అజేయు (fromtheroot chēyu చేయు) (used forchanging intransitive verbs intransitive and transitive verbs into casuative)	changed root	(1) cause to do; (2) to get it done by others.	(1) parugeththajēyu పరుగెత్తజేయు—to make one run. (2) vinajēyu వినజేయు-to make one hear (3) grahimpajēyu గ్రహింపజేయు—to make one understand.
ajālu అజాలు *or* agalugu అగలుగు	changed root (from the roots Chālu చాలు & kalugu కలుగు)	to be able to do	kottajālu కొట్టజాలు **or** kottagalugu కొట్టగలుగు -to be able to beat.
yundu యుండు (fromtheroot undu ఉండు)	Past Participle	to have already done.	Chadiviyundu చదివియుండు—to have already read.

SANDHI

In Telugu all words and terminations are divided into two main kinds called *d̄rutha prakrithikamulu* ద్రుతప్రకృతికములు and kal̄alu కళలు the former ending in న్ (n) and the letter without న్ (n).

The presence or absence of this final *(n)* న్ in a word affects the form of the last letter of that word and the first letter of the following word.

Therefore, it is necessary to know exactly to which of these two classes each word or termination belongs.. The following hints help the student to a great extent in this respect :—

1. The undermentioned groups of words and terminations are kal̄alu కళలు; *ie,* they do not end in న్ *n* :—

(a) all nouns and pronouns except *nēnu* నేను and *thānu* తాను in their original form (that is, in the nominative and vocative cases*) without the addition of any prepositions;

(b) all adjectives, including numerals;

(c) the preposition *kī* కి , *patti* పట్టి, *yokka* యొక్క, *goorchi* గూర్చి, *gurinchi* గురించి, kosamu కోసము, *dvārā* ద్వారా, *gundā* గుండా, *vīpu* వైపు, *di* ది, *vi* వి, *d̄u* డు, *nundi* నుండి, *mund̄u* ముందు.

---

*The words "man. book, he, we, it, ship" etc. are said to be in the Nominative case. The words, "oh man!, oh god! etc. are said to be in the vocative case,

(d) the adverbs *apudu* ఆపుడు, *ipudu* ఇపుడు, *epudu* ఎపుడు *ooraka* ఊరక, *ēla* ఏల, *ēni* ఏని, *kaḏa* కద, *kadā* కదా, *kāka* కాక, *kāni*, కాని,

kābatti కాబట్టి, *konchemu* (*gā*) కొంచెము (గా), mikkili మిక్కిలి,

(e) all finite verbs (of the three tenses) *not* ending in *ni* ని; or, *nu* ను.

e. g. chēsi thimi చేసితిమి.

vachiri వచ్చిరి.

thinināvu తినినావు, etc.

(f) all participles and their negatives;

e. g. chēsi చేసి

chēyaka చేయక

vini విని

vinaka వినక, etc.

2. All words and terminations not mentioned above are *drutha Prakrithikamulu* ద్రుత ప్రకృతికములు, having న్ *n* in the end.

Note the following points :—

(1) *n* న్ (ఁ) at the end of a word may be changed to ను *nu* and such ను *nu* into న్ (ఁ) *n*.

e. g. వచ్చెఁ *vachchen* = వచ్చెను *vachchenu*.
వచ్చెను *vachchenu* = వచ్చెఁ *vachchen*.

(2) న్ *n*, or ను *nu* coming at the end of a sentence may be omitted.

e. g. రాముడు వచ్చె or వచ్చెను Rāmudu vachche or vachchenu—Rāmā came.

(3) when a vowel comes immediately after న్ (౯), both the letters join together into one letter.

e. g- న్ + అ = న. (*n* + *a* = *na*). న్ *n* + ఇ i = *ni* etc.

(4) when a vowel comes immediately after ను *nu* the ఉ *u* in that ను *nu* is dropped,

e. g. వచ్చెను + అతడు = వచ్చెనతడు vaChchenu + athadu *vaChenathadu* = he came (came he)

(5) when a vowel comes immediately after the following terminations, the final vowel and the *n* న్ (౯) of the terminations, may be omitted.

అందున్ *anDun*, ఇకన్ *ikan*, చున్ *chun*, కిన్ *kin*, కున్ *kun* కొఱకున్ *korakun* నిన్ *nin* and నున్ *nun*.

e. g. అందున్ *anDun* + ఏమి *emi* — అందునేమి *anDunEmi* or అండ్ *anD* + ఏమి *Emi* — అండేమి *anDemi*.

రామునికిన్ *Ramunikin* + అపుడు *apudu* = రామునికినపుడు

Ramunikinapudu or రామునిక్ *Ramunik* + అపుడు *apudu* = రామునికపుడు *Ramunikapudu*.

Note that అందున్ *anDun* = అం + డ్ + ఉ + న్ *an* + *D* + *u* + *n*),

According to this rule, the last vowel ఉ *u* and the last న్ *n* may be omitted.

Similarly, by omiting ఇ *i* and న్ *n* in కిన్ *kin*, కి *ki* only remains.

(6) When coming immediately atter న్ (ౝ),

(a) క ka, or its formations are changed to గ ga or its formation.

చ cha	,,	,,	జ ja	,,
ట ta	,,	,,	డ da	,,
త tha	,,	,,	ద d̄a	,,
ప pa	,,	,,	బ ba	,,

e. g. వానికిౝ vanikin + కలము kalamu = వానికిౝ గలము vanikin galamu

నాకుౝ nākun + చదువు *cha*duvu = నాకుౝ జదువు nākunjaduvu

కోయుౝ kōyun + పూలు poolu = కోయుౝబూలు Koyunboolu

(b) In addition to the above change, that ౝ itself may change into ఁ, ం m, or ను nu

e. g. వ్రాయుౝ vrāyun + తప్పు thappu = వ్రాయుౝదప్పు vrāyund̄appu

or, —వ్రాయుఁదప్పు vrāyud̄appu

or, —వ్రాయుం దప్పు vrāyumd̄appu

or, —వ్రాయును దప్పు vrāyunud̄appu.

(7) when న్ (ౝ) n is immediately followed by words originally beginning with గ ga, జ ja, డ da, ద d̄a, or బ ba, or their formations, that న్ n may be changed into ం m, or ను nu; or may be omitted completely.

e. g. పోయేఁ pōyen + గుఱ్ఱము gur̄r̄amu—పోయెన్ గుఱ్ఱము = pōyen gur̄r̄amu,

or—పోయెం+గుఱ్ఱము = pōyemgur̄r̄amu,

or— పోయెను గుఱ్ఱము poyenu gur̄r̄amu

or—పోయె గుఱ్ఱము pōye gur̄r̄amu.

(8) when న్ n is immediately followed by words beginning with any consonant other than the ten mentioned in (6-a) above, that న్ n may be changed into ను nu or omitted completely.

e. g. కలిగెన్ kaligen + ధనము d̄hanamu = కలిగెన్ ధనము kaligend̄hanamu

or, కలిగెను ధనము kaligenu d̄hanamu.

or, కలిగె ధనము kalige d̄hanamu.

(9) In the above rules, wherever *n* న్ (ఁ) is followed by a consonant, it should be understood that both the letters can be joined into a compound letter as ఁ+గ=ఙ్గ nga. When a word or termination beginning with a vowel follows a finite verb ending in any vowel, or a noun ending in ఉ *u* only, the last vowel of the first word is usually dropped.

e. g. వచ్చెను+అపుడు=వచ్చెనపుడు vachchenapudu

న్ + (ఉ) + అ = న

వింటిమి+ఆ=వింటిమా vintimā

మ్ + (ఇ) + ఆ = మా

రాముడు+ఇతడే=రాముడితడే Rāmudithadē

డ్ + (ఉ) + ఇ = డి,

When a finite verb **not** ending in న్ (ౝ) *n*, ని *ni*, ను *nu*, రి *ri*, వు *vu*, రి *ri*, or రు *ru*, or any other word **not** ending in ఉ *u* or న్ (ౝ) *n*, is followed by a word beginning with a vowel, that vowel is usually **replaced by the** relative formation of య *ya*.

e. g. వచ్చెనా + ఏమి = వచ్చెనాయేమి vachchenā yēmi

నా + ఏ = నాయే

చేసిన + అతడు = చేసినయతడు chēsinayathadu

న + అ = నయ

చూడని + ఓర్పు = చూడనియోర్పు Choodaniyōrpu

ని + ఓ = నియో

బడి + అందు = బడియందు badiyandu డి + అం = డియం

When a noun or pronoun is used as the subject in a sentence (in the nominative case, without the addition of any termination), the first letter of the following word is sometimes changed from.

క *ka* or its formation to గ *ga* its formation,

చ *cha*	,,	స *sa*	,,
ట *ta*	,,	డ *da*	,,
త *tha*	,,	ద *da*	,,
ప *pa*	,,	వ *va*	,,

e. g. వాడు కొట్టెను—వాడు గొట్టెను (vadu gottenu)

బాలుడు కొనెను—బాలుడు గొనెను (bāludu gonenu)

బాలిక చదివెను—బాలిక సదివెను (bālika sadivenu)

Colloquial Telugu is prevalent in writing as well as in speaking. There are no hard and fast rules to guide the student in this respect, as there are many variations in usage from place to place in the vast Telugu-speaking area. However, the following examples may be of some help in finding out the general principles underlying this sort of expression.

చూచుచు—	Choochuchu	చూస్తూ	Choosthu
,, చున్నాము	Chunnāmu	చూస్తున్నాము	,, unnāmu
,, ,, వు	,, vu	,, వు	,, ,, vu
,, ,, రు	,, ru	,, రు	,, ,, ru
,, ,, ను	,, nu	,, ను	,, ,, nu
,, ,, డు	,, du	,, డు	,, ,, du
,, చున్నది	Chunnadi	చూస్తున్నది	Choosthunnadi
,, ,, వి	,, vi	,, వి	,, ,, vi
చేసినాడు	chēsinādu	చేశాడు	chēsādu
,, ,, వు	,, vu	,, వు	,, ,, vu
,, ,, రు	,, ru	,, రు	,, ,, ru
చేసినాను	chēsinānu	చేశాను	chēsānu
,, ,, ము	,, mu	,, ము	,, mu
చేసినది	,, nadi	చేసింది	chēsindi
,, ,, వి	,, vi	చేసినవి	chēsinavi
పోయెదను	pōyedanu	పోతాను	pōthānu
,, ము	,, mu	,, ము	,, mu
,, వు	,, vu	,, వు	,, vu
,, రు	,, ru	,, రు	,, ru
పోవును	pōvunu	,, డు	,, du

పోవును (స్త్రీ. నపుం)	pōvunu	పోతుంది	pōthundi
చూచుట	choochuta	చూడడం	choodadam
చూచుటకు	,, ku	చూడటానికి	,, tāniki
వ్రాయుము	vrāyumu	వ్రాయి	vrāyi
చేయను	chēyanu	చెయ్యను	cheyyanu
వచ్చినచో	vachchinachō	వస్తే	vasthē
రావలెను	rāvalenu	రావాలి	rāvāli

LESSCN 11

Vocabulary

THE UNIVERSE

Bhagavanthudu భగవంతుడు, devudu దేవుడు —God

srushti సృష్టి—creation

srushtikartha సృష్టికర్త—creator

visvamu విశ్వము—universe

prapanchamu ప్రపంచము—world

svargamu స్వర్గము—heaven

narakamu నరకము—hell

Chukka చుక్క, nakshathramu నక్షత్రము —star

ākasamu ఆకాశము—sky

rāsi chakramu రాశి చక్రము—zodiac

The planetary system

Sooryudu సూర్యుడు—Sun

Chandrudu చంద్రుడు—Moon

Kujudu కుజుడు Mars

Budhudu బుధుడు—Mercury

Guruvu గురువు—Jupiter

Sukrudu శుక్రుడు—Venus

Sani శని—Saturn

thokachukka తోకచుక్క —comet

ulka ఉల్క —meteor

grahamu గ్రహము—planet

upagrahamu ఉపగ్రహము—satellite

grahañamu గ్రహణము—eclipse

bhoomi భూమి—the earth

The Earth.

nēla నేల—land

samud̄ramu సముద్రము—sea

mahā samud̄ramu మహా సముద్రము—ocean

d̄hruvamu ధ్రువము—pole

enda ఎండ—sun (heat & light)

vennela వెన్నెల—moonlight

velathuru వెలుతురు }—light
prakāsamu ప్రకాశము }

vēdi (mi) వేడి (మి)—heat

kirañamu కిరణము—ray

needa నీడ—shade

chāya ఛాయ—shadow

manC̄hu మంచు—snow

manC̄hu gadda మంచు గడ్డ—ice

vāna వాన }—rain
varshamu వర్షము }

konda కొండ—hill

parvathamu పర్వతము—mountain

gutta గుట్ట—hillock

vāthāvarañamu వాతావరణము—atmosphere

sēthōshna sthhithi శీతోష్ణస్థితి—climate

gāli గాలి
vāyuvu వాయువు } —wind, air

gālivāna గాలివాన
thupānu తుపాను } —storm

bhookampamu భూకంపము—earth quake

agni parvathamu అగ్ని పర్వతము—volcano

mēghamu మేఘము
mabbu మబ్బు } —cloud

ur̄umu ఉఱుము—thunder

mer̄upu మెఱుపు—lightning

pidugu పిడుగు—thunderbolt

vid̄yuc̄hhchakthi విద్యుచ్ఛక్తి—electricity

nippu నిప్పు
agni అగ్ని } —fire

neeru నీరు
jalamu జలము } —water

manchi neeru మంచి నీరు—fresh water

mīd̄ānamu మైదానము—plain

peethabhoomi పీఠభూమి—plateau

lōya లోయ—valley

guha గుహ—cave

cher̄uvu చెఱువు—tank

sarassu సరస్సు—lake

kāluva కాలువ—canal

nad̄i నది—river

Directions.

thoorpu తూర్పు—east
āgnēyamu ఆగ్నేయము—south-east
ḋakshinamu దక్షిణము—south
nīrrithi నైరృతి—south-west
padamara పడమర—west
vayuvyamu వాయువ్యము—north-west
uththaramu ఉత్తరము—north
eeŝānyamu ఈశాన్యము—north east
ḋikku దిక్కు—direction

Time.

kālamu కాలము—time
kshañamu క్షణము—second
nimusamu నిముసము } —minute
nimishamu నిమిషము }
aranimusamu అరనిముసము—half a minute
pāvu ganta పావుగంట—quarter of an hour
araganta అరగంట—half an hour
muppāvuganta ముప్పావుగంట—three quarters of an hour
ganta గంట—hour
jāmu జాము—three hours
pagalu పగలు—day time
rāthri రాత్రి—night
ḋinamu దినము } —a day
rōju రోజు }
vāramu వారము—week
vārānthamu వారాంతము—week-end

pakshamu పక్షము—fortnight

Śuklapakshamu శుక్లపక్షము
Śuḍḍa ,, శుద్ధ ,, } —bright fortnight

krushṇapakshamu కృష్ణపక్షము
bahuḷa ,, బహుళపక్షము } —dark fortnight

poorṇima పూర్ణిమ—full moon

amāvāsya అమావాస్య—new-moon

nela నెల—month

ruthuvu ఋతువు—season (two-monthly)

vēsavikālamu వేసవికాలము—Summer

varshākālamu వర్షాకాలము—Rainy season

Seethakālamu శీతకాలము
Chali ,, చలి ,, } —winter

vasanthakālamu వసంతకాలము—Spring

ēdu ఏడు
samvathsaramu సంవత్సరము } —year

ugāḍi ఉగాది—New year's-day

thellavārajāmu తెల్లవారుజాము— early hours of the day (before sunrise.)

sooryōḍayamu సూర్యోదయము—sun-rise

sooryāsthamayamu సూర్యాస్తమయము—sunset

uḍayamu ఉదయము
proḍḍuna ప్రొద్దున } —morning

maḍhyāhnamu మధ్యాహ్నము—noon, midday

sāyankālamu సాయంకాలము—evening

arḍharāthri అర్ధరాత్రి—midnight

eenela ఈనెల—instant (this month)

ellundi ఎల్లుండి—day-after tomorrow

ninna నిన్న—yesterday

monna మొన్న—day before yesterday

marunādu మరునాడు—next day

krinḍatirōju క్రిందటిరోజు—previous day

nēdu నేడు
ee rōju ఈరోజు } —today

rēpu రేపు—tomorrow

Days of the week

ādivāramu
ఆదివారము } —Sunday

sōmavāramu సోమవారము—Monday

mangaḷavāramu మంగళవారము—Tuesday

buḍhavāramu బుధవారము—Wednesday

guruvāramu గురువారము—Thursday

śukravāramu శుక్రవారము—Friday

śanivāramu శనివారము—Saturday

Minerals.

gani గని—mine

bangāramu బంగారము—gold

venḍi వెండి—silver

rāgi రాగి—copper

iththadi ఇత్తడి—brass

kanČhu కంచు—bronze

nĕlabŏggu నీలబొగ్గు—coal

vajramu వజ్రము—diamond

kempu కెంపు—ruby

paČhČha పచ్చ—emerald

pagaḍamu పగడము—coral

thruppu త్రుప్పు—rust

chilumu చిలుము—verdigris

mīlathuththamu మైలతుత్తము—(blue) vītriol

sindooramu సిందూరము—vermillion

abhrakamu అభ్రకము
kāki bangaramu కాకి బంగారము } — mica

pāḍarasamu పాదరసము—mercury

inumu ఇనుము—iron

ukku ఉక్కు—steel

seesamu సీసము—lead

thagaramu తగరము—tin

thuththunāgamu తుత్తునాగము—zinc

pushyarāgamu పుష్యరాగము—topaz

neelamu నీలము—sapphire

sphatikamu స్ఫటికము—crystal

muthyamu ముత్యము—pearl

khanijamu ఖనిజము—mineral

gandhakamu గంధకము—sulphur

Numerals.

(a) Cardinals :

1 ౧ okati ఒకటి—(one)
2 ౨ rendu రెండు—(two)
3 ౩ moodu మూడు—(three)
4 ౪ nālugu నాలుగు—(four)
5 ౫ Īd̄u **or** ayid̄u అయిదు
6 ౬ āṟu ఆఱు
7 ౭ ēdu ఏడు
8 ౮ enimid̄i ఎనిమిది
9 ౯ thommid̄i తొమ్మిది
0 ౧౦ pad̄i పది
1 ౧౧ pad̄akondu పదకొండు
2 ౧౨ pandrendu పండ్రెండు
3 ౧౩ pad̄amoodu పదమూడు
4 ౧౪ pad̄unālugu పదునాలుగు
5 ౧౫ pad̄unĪd̄u పదునైదు
6 ౧౬ pad̄unāṟu పదునాఱు
7 ౧౭ pad̄unēdu పదునేడు
8 ౧౮ pad̄unenimid̄i పదునెనిమిది
9 ౧౯ pandommidi పందొమ్మిది
0 ౨౦ iruvad̄i ఇరువది
1 ౨౧ iruvad̄i okati ఇరువది ఒకటి

22 ౨౨ ,, rendu ,, రెండు
23 ౨౩ ,, moodu ,, మూడు
24 ౨౪ ,, nālugu ,, నాలుగు
25 ౨౫ ,, Īdu ,, ఐదు
26 ౨౬ ,, āṟu ,, ఆఱు
27 ౨౭ ,, ēdu ,, ఏడు
28 ౨౮ ,, enimid̄i ,, ఎనిమిది
29 ౨౯ ,, thommid̄i ,, తొమ్మిది
30 ౩౦ muppad̄i ముప్పది
31 ౩౧ muppad̄i okati ముప్పది ఒకటి
32 ౩౨ muppad̄i rendu ముప్పది రెండు
40 ౪౦ { నలుబది nalubad̄i / నలువది naluvad̄i }
50 ౫౦ ఏబది ēbad̄i
60 ౬౦ అరువది aruvad̄i
70 ౭౦ డెబ్బది debbad̄i
80 ౮౦ ఎనుబది enubad̄i
90 ౯౦ తొంబది thombad̄i
100 ౧౦౦ { నూరు nooru / వంద vand̄a }
101 ౧౦౧ నూట ఒకటి noota okati
102 ౧౦౨ నూట రెండు noota rendu
110 ౧౧౦ నూట పది noota pad̄i

190	౧౯౦	నూటతొంబది nootathombad̄i
199	౧౯౯	నూటతొంబదితొమ్మిది nootathombad̄i thommid̄i
200	౨౦౦	రెండువందలు renduvand̄alu ఇన్నూరు innooru
201	౨౦౧	రెండువందలఒకటి renduvand̄alaokati ఇన్నూటఒకటి innotaokati
202	౨౦౨	రెండువందలరెండు renduvand̄ala rendu ఇన్నూటరెండు innootarendu
300	౩౦౦	మూడువందలు mooduvand̄alu మున్నూరు munnooru
301	౩౦౧	మూడువందలఒకటి mooduvand̄ala okati మున్నూటఒకటి munnootaokati
400	౪౦౦	నాలుగువందలు nāluguvand̄alu నన్నూరు nannooru
500	౫౦౦	అయిదువందలు ayid̄uvand̄alu అయిదునూర్లు ayid̄unoorlu
600	౬౦౦	ఆరువందలు (నూర్లు) āruvand̄alu (noorlu)
700	౭౦౦	ఏడువందలు (నూర్లు) ēduvand̄alu (noorlu)
800	౮౦౦	ఎనిమిదివందలు (నూర్లు) enimid̄ivand̄alu (noorlu)
900	౯౦౦	తొమ్మిదివందలు (నూర్లు) thommid̄i vand̄alu (noorlu)
999	౯౯౯	తొమ్మిదివందల (నూర్ల) తొంబదితొమ్మిది thommid̄ivand̄ala (noorla) thombad̄ithommid̄i

1,000	౧,౦౦౦	వెయ్యి veyyi వేయి vēyi
1,001	౧,౦౦౧	వెయ్యి ఒకటి veyyi okati
1,100	౧,౧౦౦	వెయ్యిఒకవంద veyyiokavanda
2,000	౨,౦౦౦	రెండువేలు renduvēlu
3,000	౩,౦౦౦	మూడువేలు mooduvēlu
4,000	౪,౦౦౦	నాలుగువేలు nāluguvēlu
5,000	౫,౦౦౦	అయిదువేలు ayiduvēlu
6,000	౬,౦౦౦	ఆరువేలు āruvēlu
7,000	౭,౦౦౦	ఏడువేలు ēduvēlu
8,000	౮,౦౦౦	ఎనిమిదివేలు enimidivēlu
9,000	౯,౦౦౦	తొమ్మిదివేలు thommidivēlu
10,000	౧౦,౦౦౦	పదివేలు padivēlu
20,000	౨౦,౦౦౦	ఇరువదివేలు iruvadivēlu
1,00,000	౧,౦౦,౦౦౦	(ఒక) లక్ష (oka) laksha
2,00,000	౨,౦౦,౦౦౦	రెండులక్షలు rendulakshalu
10,00,000	౧౦,౦౦,౦౦౦	పదిలక్షలు padilakshalu
1,00,00,000	౧,౦౦,౦౦,౦౦౦	(ఒక) కోటి (oka) kōti
2,00,00,000	౨,౦౦,౦౦,౦౦౦	రెండుకోట్లు rendukōtlu
10,00,00,000	౧౦,౦౦,౦౦,౦౦౦	పదికోట్లు padikōtlu
20,00,00,000	౨౦,౦౦,౦౦,౦౦౦	ఇరువదికోట్లు iruvadikōtlu

The first cardinal ఒకటి okati means number one. But in the sense of the word "single" (a or an), ఒక oka is used. Thus, when you count one, two, three, etc., the Telugu equivalents would be ఒకటి okati రెండు rendu, మూడు

moodu, etc. But, when you say one book, two books etc., they are to be translated as "ఒక పుస్తకము oka pusthakamu, రెండు పుస్తకములు rendu pusthakamulu," etc. These cardinals are used for nouns other than personal,

(b) For personal nouns, there are special cardinals upto four.

1. ఒకడు okadu or ఒకరు okaru (a term used respcetfully, = one person (both genders)

2. ఇద్దఱు iddaṟu = two persons

3. ముగ్గురు mugguru = three persons

4. నలుగురు naluguru / నలువురు naluvuru = four persons

Thereafter, the personal cardinals are formed by adding the termination మంది mandi (or గురు guru) to the ordinary cardinals given above.

5. అయిదుమంది ayidumandi = five persons

6. ఆరుమంది ārumandi = six ,,

10. పదిమంది padimandi = ten ,,

100. నూరుమంది noorumandi / వందమంది vandamandi = hundred persons

1000. వేయి (వెయ్యి) మంది vēyi (veyyi) mandi = thousnd persons etc., etc.

The words నలుగురు naluguru and పదిమంది padimandi are idomatically used to denote the people at large.

e. g. నలుగురు (or పదిమంది) నవ్వేదరు naluguru (or pad̄i-mand̄i) navved̄aru = people will laugh (at...)

(c) **Multiplicatives** are formed as follows by **adding** రెట్లు *retlu* to the cardinals.

(a) { రెట్టింపు rettimpu / రెండురెట్లు renduretlu } = double, twofold

మూడురెట్లు mooduretlu = triple, three fold

నాలుగురెట్లు nāluguretlu = quadruple, four fold

etc., etc.

(d) **Personal multiplicatives** are formed by adding మంది *mand̄i* to the ordinary multiplicatives given in **(c) above** రెట్టింపుమంది rettimpumand̄i = double the number **of persons** మూడురెట్లమంది mooduretlamand̄i = triple. etc.,

(e) Ordinals are formed by adding అవ ava to the **cardinals** given in (a) above. However, the first ordinal **is** ఒకటవ **okatava** or మొదటి mod̄ati.

రెండు + అవ = రెండవ (Art 21) rendava = second

మూడు + అవ = మూడవ moodava = third

నాలుగు + అవ = నాలుగవ nālugava } fourth (నాలవ nālava
నాల్గు + అవ = నాల్గవ nālgava } also is used.

అయిదు + అవ = అయిదవ ayid̄ava } = fifth
ఐదు + అవ = ఐదవ īd̄ava }

ఆరు + అవ = ఆరవ ārava = sixth

etc. etc.

These ordinals are used for personal nouns **also.**

e. g. పదవ కలము padāva kalamu = tenth pen
పదవ మనుష్యుడు padāva manushyudu = **tenth man**

(f) If the term వంతు *vanthu* is added to the **ordinals** iven in (e) above, it expresses the reciprocals **(fractions)** thereof.

e. g. ఐదవ వంతు īdava vanthu = one fifth = $\frac{1}{5}$

The fraction $\frac{4}{5}$ is read in Telugu as అయిదింట నాలుగు వంతులు ayidinta nālugu **vanthulu**

" $\frac{6}{7}$ " " ఏడింట ఆరు వంతులు ēdinta āru **vanthulu**

(g) Numerical Adverbs :—

okasāri ఒకసారి—once
okēsāri ఒకేసారి—only once
rendu sārlu రెండు సార్లు—twice
rendē sārlu రెండే సార్లు—only twice
moodu sārlu మూడు సార్లు— thrice
moodē sārlu మూడే సార్లు—only thrice
nālugu sārlu నాలుగు సార్లు—four times
nālugē sārlu నాలుగే సార్లు—only four times

Society.

lingamu లింగము—sex

manushyudu మనుష్యుడు
purushudu పురుషుడు } —man

sthree స్త్రీ—woman

śiśuvu శిశువు—child, baby, Infant

pasivādu పసివాడు—male child

pasipilla పసిపిల్ల—female child

pillavādu పిల్లవాడు
bāludu బాలుడు } —boy

pilla పిల్ల
ādapilla ఆడపిల్ల
bālika బాలిక } —girl

yuvakudu యువకుడు—a young man

yuvathi యువతి—a young woman

peddavādu పెద్ద వాడు—an adult male; elderly man

peddadī (female) పెద్దది—an adult female; elderly woman

vriddudu వృద్ధుడు
musalivadu ముసలివాడు } —old man

vriddhurālu వృద్ధురాలు
musalamma ముసలమ్మ } —old woman

thallidandrulu తల్లిదండ్రులు—parents

amma అమ్మ
thalli తల్లి } —mother

thandri తండ్రి
ayya అయ్య
nāyanna నాయన } —father

thātha తాత—grand-father

muththāta ముత్తాత—great-grand father

avva అవ్వ—grand-mother

ammamma అమ్మమ్మ—mother's mother

nāyanamma నాయనమ్మ—father's mother

kumārudu కుమారుడు
puthrudu పుత్రుడు } —son
koduku కొడుకు

koothuru కూతురు
kumārthe కుమార్తె } —daughter

manumadu మనుమడు—grand-son

manumarālu మనుమరాలు—grand-daughter

munimanumadu మునిమనుమడు—great-grand-son

guruvu గురువు—teacher

Sishyudu శిష్యుడు—disciple

pempudu koduku పెంపుడు కొడుకు—adopted son

pempudu koothuru పెంపుడుకూతురు—adopted daughter

sōdari సోదరి—sister

chellelu చెల్లెలు—younger sister

akka అక్క, appa అప్ప—elder sister

anna అన్న—elder brother

thammudu తమ్ముడు—younger brother

annadammulu అన్నదమ్ములు—brothers

sōdarudu సోదరుడు—brother

pedathalli పెదతల్లి—maternal aunt (elder)

pinathalli పినతల్లి— (younger)

pedathandri పెదతండ్రి-father's elder brother } (paternal
chinathandri చినతండ్రి ,, younger brother } uncle)

mēna-māma మేనమామ—mother's brother (maternal uncle)

mēnalludu మేనల్లుడు —a man's sister's son or a woman's brother's son

mênakōdalu మేనకోడలు—a man's sister's daughter or a woman's brother's daughter

mēnatha మేనత్త—father's sister

māma (yya) మామ (య్య)—father-in-law

bāva బావ — brother-in-law; paternal aunt's son; maternal uncle's son

vadine వదినె–sister-in-law; paternal aunt's daughter; maternal uncle's daughter

maradalu మఱదలు–younger brother's wife, or, wife's sister

aththa (yya) అత్త (య్య)—mother-in-law

alludu అల్లుడు—son-in-law

kōdalu కోడలు—daughter-in-law

viyyapurālu వియ్యపురాలు—mother of the son-in-law or daughter-in-law

viyyankudu వియ్యంకుడు—father of the son-in-law or daughter-in-law

gnāthi జ్ఞాతి
dāyādi దాయాది } —kinsman

brahmachāri బ్రహ్మచారి—bachelor

kanya కన్య—virgin

vidhava విధవ—widow

vidhurudu విధురుడు—widower

magadu మగడు
bhartha భర్త } —husband

bhārya భార్య—wife

savathi సవతి —co-wife

savathi-thalli సవతితల్లి—step-mother

kutumbamu కుటుంబము—family

poorveekulu పూర్వీకులు—ancestors

pendli పెండ్లి
vivāhamu వివాహము } —marriage

pendlikoduku పెండ్లికొడుకు
varudu వరుడు } —bride-groom

pendlikoothuru పెండ్లికూతురు
vadhuvu వధువు } —bride

pendlivāru పెండ్లివారు—bridal party

katnamu కట్నము—dowry

kānukalu కానుకలు—presents

oorēgimpu ఊరేగింపు—procession

bandhuvu బంధువు
Chuttamu చుట్టము } —relative

chuttarikamu చుట్టరికము
bandhuthvamu బంధుత్వము } —relationship

snēhithudu స్నేహితుడు
mithramu మిత్రము } —friend
mithrudu మిత్రుడు

virōdhi విరోధి
Sathruvu శత్రువు } —enemy
pagavādu పగవాడు

yajamāni యజమాని
prabhuvu ప్రభువు } —lord

kouludāru కౌలుదారు
kirāyadāru కిరాయదారు } —tenant

gumāsthā గుమాస్తా—clerk

poruguvādu పొరుగువాడు—neighbour

bānisa బానిస—slave

svathanthrudu స్వతంత్రుడు—free-man

sēvakudu సేవకుడు—servant

panikaththe పనికత్తె—servant maid

bhāgyavanthudu భాగ్యవంతుడు
dhanikudu ధనికుడు } —richman

beedarālu బీదరాలు
pēdarālu పేదరాలు } —poor woman

beedavādu బీదవాడు
pēdavādu పేదవాడు } —poor man

bichchagādu బిచ్చగాడు
yāchakudu యాచకుడు } —beggar

bhāgyamu భాగ్యము
īsvaryamu ఐశ్వర్యము } — prosperity riches

pēdarikamu పేదఱికము—poverty

The Human Body.

sareeramu శరీరము
dēhamu దేహము } —body

thala తల—head

ventrukalu వెంట్రుకలు—hair

purre పుఱ్ఱె—skull

medadu మెదడు—brain

nuduru నుదురు—forehead

mukhamu ముఖము—face

kannu కన్ను—eye

kanubomma కనుబొమ్మ—eyebrow

kanureppa కనురెప్ప—eye lid

kantipāpa కంటిపాప—pupil of the eye

chevi చెవి—ear

mukku ముక్కు—nose

mukkuranđhramulu ముక్కురంధ్రములు—nostrils

nōru నోరు—mouth

nāluka నాలుక—tongue

pandlu పండ్లు—teeth

kondanāluka కొండనాలుక—uvula

peđavi పెదవి—lip

gonthu గొంతు—throat

đouda దౌడ
bugga బుగ్గ } —cheek, jaw

meesamulu మీసములు—mustaches

gađdamu గడ్డము—chin, beard

meda మెడ—neck

r̄ommu రొమ్ము—chest

c̄hannulu చన్నులు—breast

bhujamu భుజము—shoulder

chēyi చేయి—hand

mōchēyi మోచేయి—elbow

ar̄achēyi అరచేయి--palm

c̄hanka చంక—arm-pit

man̄ikattu మణికట్టు—wrist

pidikili పిడికిలి—fist

vrēlu వ్రేలు—finger

botanavrēlu బొటనవ్రేలు—thumb

rakthanāl̄amu రక్తనాళము—vein or artery

emuka ఎముక—bone

gōru గోరు—nail

kadupu కడుపు
potta పొట్ట } —stomach

booddu బొడ్డు—navel

prēgulu ప్రేగులు—intestines

charmamu చర్మము
thōlu తోలు } —skin

oopirithiththulu ఊపిరితిత్తులు—lungs

gunde గుండె—heart

nadumu నడుము—waist

rakthamu రక్తము—blood

mamsamu మాంసము } —flesh
kanda కండ

naramu నరము—nerve

plcehamu ప్లీహము – liver

yakriththu యకృత్తు—spleen

veepu వీపు—back

vennemuka వెన్నముక—backbone

thoda తొడ—thigh

pikka పిక్క—calf of the leg

odi ఒడి—lap

mōkālu మోకాలు—knee

kālu కాలు—leg

cheelamanda చీలమండ—ankle

pādamu పాదము—foot

madama మడమ—heel

(kāli) botanavrēlu (కాలి) బొటనవ్రేలు—toe

arikālu అఱికాలు—sole (of the foot)

yoni యోని—the female sex organ

lingamu లింగము—the male sex organ

vrishaṅamulu వృషణములు—testicles

asanamu ఆసనము } —anus
muddi ముడ్డి

chemata చెమట—sweat

malamu మలము—"stools"

moothramu మూత్రము—urine

Sukramu శుక్రము—sperm

ummi ఉమ్మి } —Saliva
lālājalamu లాలాజలము

andamu అందము—beauty

andaviheenamu అందవిహీనము—ugliness.

Bodily Functions & Disorders.

ārōgyamu ఆరోగ్యము—health

anārōgyamu అనారోగ్యము—ill-health

rōgamu రోగము } —sickness, disease
jabbu జబ్బు
vyādhi వ్యాధి

mandu మందు } —medicine
oushadhamu ఔషధము

thaththvamu తత్త్వము—constitution

vinuta వినుట—hearing

vāsana C̄hooC̄huta వాసన చూచుట—smelling

thākuta తాకుట—touch

ruchi రుచి—taste

mātalu మాటలు—speach

māta మాట—word

S̄vāsa శ్వాస } —breath
oopiri ఊపిరి }

jeerñamu జీర్ణము—digestion

nadaka నడక—walking

gruddi గ్రుడ్డి—blind

kunti కుంటి—lame

kāramu కారము—hot, pungent

uppana ఉప్పన—saltish taste

ogaru ఒగరు—acrid

noppi నొప్పి—pain

thalanoppi తలనొప్పి—head-ache

manta మంట—burning sensation

kandlakalaka కండ్లకలక—opthalmia, sore eyes

jalubu జలుబు, padiS̄emu పడిశెము—coryza, cold

d̄aggu దగ్గు—cough

vikāramu వికారము—giddiness

vānthi వాంతి—vomit

ajeernamu అజీర్ణము—indigestion

ākalilēkapŌvuta ఆకలి లేక పోవుట—dyspepsia

virēchana bad̄hd̄hakamu విరేచనబద్ధకము—constipation

virēchanamulu విరేచనములు—diarrhoea

raktha ,, రక్త ,, —dysentery

C̄hoopu చూపు—sight

mooga మూగ—dumb

naththi నత్తి—stammering

cheviti చెవిటి—deaf

aviti అవిటి—cripple

mellakannu మెల్లకన్ను—squint eye

ākali ఆకలి—hunger

d̄āhamu దాహము } —thirst
d̄appi దప్పి }

S̄abd̄amu శబ్దము } —sound
d̄hvani ధ్వని }

suvāsana సువాసన—good smell

d̄urvāsana దుర్వాసన—bad smell

chēd̄u చేదు—bitter, bitterness

pulupu పులుపు—sourness

theepi తీపి—sweetness

chemata చెమట—sweat

moorchha మూర్ఛ—fainting

bonguru gonthu బొంగురు గొంతు—hoarse voice

kshaya క్షయ—T. B. (consumption)

nanju నంజు
neeru నీరు } —dropsy

thāmara తామర—ringworm

kushtu కుష్టు—leprosy

maśoochi మశూచి—small pox

pakshavāthamu పక్షవాతము—paralysis

thimmiri తిమ్మిరి—numbness

balaheenatha బలహీనత—weakness

bhāramu భారము
baruvu బరువు } —heaviness

ātalamma ఆటలమ్మ—chicken-pox

chinnabidda guṇamu చిన్నబిడ్డగుణము—convulsions

mahāmāri మహామారి—plague

sandhi సంధి—delirium

magatha మగత—coma

cheemu చీము—puss

kuṟupu కురుపు—boil

vāpu వాపు—swelling

chikithsa చికిత్స—treatment

nayamaguta నయమగుట
kuduruta కుదురుట } cure

thirugabettuta తిరుగబెట్టుట—relapse

kusuma కుసుమ—lucorrhoea

snānamu స్నానము—bath

sukharŌgamu సుఖరోగము—venereal disease

pathhyamu పథ్యము—good diet

apathyamu అపథ్యము—bad diet

mand̄u మందు—medicine

muttu ముట్టు—menses

garbhini గర్భిణి—pregnant

prasoothi ప్రసూతి—delivery

ben̄uku బెణుకు—sprain

gāyamu గాయము—wound

pundu పుండు—ulcer

d̄urad̄a దురద—itching

gajji గజ్జి—itch

chāvu చావు
mrithyuvu మృత్యువు } —death

prān̄amu ప్రాణము—life

pongu పొంగు—measles

vishoochi విషూచి—cholera

pichchi పిచ్చి—insanity

jvaramu జ్వరము—fever

Mind & Soul.

manassu మనస్సు—mind
āthma ఆత్మ—soul
ālōchana ఆలోచన—thinking
thrupthi తృప్తి—satisfaction
santhōshamu సంతోషము-gladness
vichāramu విచారము } —sorrow
dukhamu దుఃఖము }
sukhamu సుఖము—happiness
kashtamu కష్టము—trouble
kōpamu కోపము—anger
asooya అసూయ—jealousy
āSa ఆశ—greed, hope
nirāSa నిరాశ—hopelessness
athyāSa అత్యాశ—to much greed
budhi బుద్ధి—faculty
jnānamu జ్ఞానము—wisdom
ajnānamu అజ్ఞానము—ignorance
uddēSyamu ఉద్దేశ్యము—idea
abhiprāyamu అభిప్రాయము-opinion
lakshyamu లక్ష్యము—aim
yukthi యుక్తి—wit, device

upāyamu ఉపాయము—plan
kāraṇamu కారణము—reason, cause
kāryamu కార్యము పని—pani-work
chapalachiththamu చపలచిత్తము—indecisiveness
nirṇayamu నిర్ణయము—decision
sathyamu సత్యము } —truth
nijamu నిజము }
abadhdhamu అబద్ధము } lie, untruth
asathyamu అసత్యము }
porabātu పొరబాటు—oversight
thappu తప్పు—error
Sradhdha శ్రద్ధ—care, attention
uthsāhamu ఉత్సాహము—zeal
marapu మఱపు—forgetfulness

jnapthi జ్ఞప్తి—memory

prēma [ప్రేమ—love

snēhamu స్నేహము—friendship

guñamu గుణము—quality

suguñamu సుగుణము—good quality

ḍurguñamu దుర్గుణము—bad quality

bhayamu భయము—fear

hāsyamu హాస్యము—humour

ooha ఊహా—opinion, imagination

parichayamu పరిచయము—familiarity

nammakamu నమ్మకము—belief

viśvāsamu విశ్వాసము—faith

ishtamu ఇష్టము—liking

asahyamu అసహ్యము—dislike

kōrika కోరిక—desire

āṇḍōlana ఆందోళన—anxiety

āthuratha ఆతురత—hurry

siggu సిగ్గు—shame

maryāḍa మర్యాద—politeness, courtesy

amaryāḍa అమర్యాద—impoliteness

pavithratha పవిత్రత—purity

apavithratha అపవిత్రత—impurity

śeelamu శీలము—chastity

pāpamu పాపము—sin

puñyamu పుణ్యము—result of a good act

ḍānamu దానము—charity

ḍharmamu ధర్మము—duty

d̄aya దయ—pity
sānubhoothi సానుభూతి—sympathy
āthid̄hyamu ఆతిథ్యము—hospitality
vid̄hēyatha విధేయత—obedience
Šānthamu శాంతము—piety
ōrpu ఓర్పు—patience
bhakthi భక్తి—devotion
paSchāththāpamu పశ్చాత్తాపము—repentence
Īkamathyamu ఐకమత్యము—unity
virōd̄hamu విరోధము—enimity
anukoolamu అనుకూలము—advantage; for
prathikoolamu ప్రతికూలము—disadvantage
gouravamu గౌరవము—honour
agouravamu అగౌరవము—dishonour
krutha*jhna*tha కృతజ్ఞత—gratitude
krūtha*ghna*tha కృతఘ్నత—ingratitude
amāyikathvamu అమాయికత్వము—innocence
ādambaramu ఆడంబరము—show
nirādambaramu నిరాడంబరము—simplicity
nērpu నేర్పు—skill
anubhavamu అనుభవము—experience
abhyāsamu అభ్యాసము—practice
dhīryamu ధైర్యము—courage
sāhasamu సాహసము—daringness
alavātu అలవాటు—habit
anumānamu అనుమానము—presumption
sand̄ēhamu సందేహము—doubt

d̄ōshamu దోషము
aparād̄hamu అపరాధము } —misdeed

nēramu నేరము—crime

paga పగ—vengeance

egathāli ఎగతాళి
vekkirintha వెక్కిరింత } —mocking

thiraskāramu తిరస్కారము—refusal

vyabhichāramu వ్యభిచారము—debauchery

d̄ongathanamu దొంగతనము—theft

garvamu గర్వము—pride

vinayamu వినయము—submissiveness

mōsamu మోసము—deceipt

ajāgratha అజాగ్రత—negligence

lubd̄hathvamu లుబ్ధత్వము—miserliness

d̄urvyayamu దుర్వ్యయము—prodigality

pakshapāthamu పక్షపాతము—partiality

nishpakshapāthamu నిష్పక్షపాతము—impartiality

thrāgudu త్రాగుడు—drinking

thrāgubōthu త్రాగుబోతు—drunkard

mōhamu మోహము—love; passion

avamānamu అవమానము—insult

mēlu మేలు—good

keedu కీడు—harm

abhimānamu అభిమానము—attachment

kroorathvamu క్రూరత్వము—cruelty

hathya హత్య—murder

āthmahathya ఆత్మహత్య—suicide

āchāramu ఆచారము—custom, practice

Food & Drink.

āhāramu ఆహారము—food

māmsamu మాంసము—meat

annamu అన్నము—boiled rice

koora కూర—curry

sākāhaarmu శాకాహారము—vegetarian meals

māmsāhāramu మాంసాహారము—non-vegetarian meals

pālu పాలు—milk

rotte రొట్టె—bread

pindi పిండి—flour

panchadāra పంచదార
chakkera చక్కెర —sugar

pachchadi పచ్చడి—chutney

ooragāya ఊరగాయ—pickles

pandlu పండ్లు—fruits

kāya కాయ—raw fruit

dōrakāya దోరకాయ—half-ripe fruit

pulusu పులుసు—soup

pappu పప్పు—boiled pulses (dholl)

nēyi నేయి—clarified butter (ghee)

majjiga మజ్జిగ
challa చల్ల —butter milk

chāru చారు—light soup

perugu పెరుగు—curd

noone నూనె—oil

manchinoone మంచినూనె
nuvvulanoone నువ్వులనూనె } —gingily oil (sweet oil)

vērusanaganoone వేరుశనగనూనె—groundnut oil

kobbarinoone కొబ్బరినూనె—coçoanut oil

āmud̄amu ఆముదము—castor oil

thạmulapāku తములపాకు—betal leaf

vakkalu వక్కలు
pōkalu పోకలు } —arecanuts

sunnamu సున్నము—lime

karpooramu కర్పూరము—camphor

kumkumapuvvu కుంకుమపువ్వు—saffron

ēlakulu ఏలకులు—cardamum

lavangamulu లవంగములు—clove

sugand̄ha d̄ravyamulu సుగంధ ద్రవ్యములు—spices

d̄ālchinachekka దాల్చినచెక్క
lavngapatta లవంగపట్ట } —cinnamon

jājikāya జాజికాయ—nutmeg

jāpathri జాపత్రి—mace

sōpu సోపు—anise

pindivanta పిండివంట—eatables prepared with flour and ghee or oil

pākamu పాకము—jelly-like preparation of sugar or jaggery

patika bellamu పటిక బెల్లము—sugar-candy

pānakamu పానకము—syrup

mirapakāyalu మిరపకాయలు—chillies (dried) (red pepper)
pesalu పెసలు—green gram
kand̄ulu కందులు—red gram
minumulu మినుములు—black gram
Šanagalu శనగలు—bengal gram
vērušanagalu వేరుశనగలు—ground-nut
āvālu ఆవాలు—mustard
menthulu మెంతులు—fenugreek
jeelakar̄r̄a జీలకర్ర—cummin seed
ullipāyalu ఉల్లిపాయలు—onions
vellulli వెల్లుల్లి—garlic
inguva ఇంగువ—asafoetida
d̄haniyālu ధనియాలు—coriander
pasupu పసుపు—turmeric
bellamu బెల్లము—jaggery
biyyamu బియ్యము—rice
gōd̄humalu గోధుమలు—wheat
jonnalu జొన్నలు—millet
mokkajonnalu మొక్కజొన్నలు—corn
pappulu పప్పులు—pulses
saggubiyyamu సగ్గుబియ్యము—sago
nuvvulu నువ్వులు—sesame
miriyālu మిరియాలు—pepper
allamu అల్లము—ginger
Šontthi శొంఠి—dried ginger

grudlu గ్రుడ్లు—eggs

chēpalu చేపలు—fishes

sona సొన—yolk

mukka ముక్క—piece

mud̄d̄a ముద్ద—morsel

venna వెన్న—butter

meegada మీగడ – cream

junnu జున్ను—cheese

pēlālu పేలాలు—friend paddy or millet

c̄halid̄i చలిది (annamu అన్నము) } –food kept overnight
c̄had̄d̄i చద్ది ,,

bhōjanamu భోజనము—meal

manchineeru మంచినీరు—fresh-water

vaddana వడ్డన—serving food

māru మారు—second course of a meal

phalāhāramu ఫలాహారము–fruit diet (colloquially used for "tiffin")

upāhāramu ఉపాహారము—tiffin

bādamu బాదము—almond

jeedipappu జీడిపప్పు—cashewnut

batāneelu బటానీలు—peas

atukulu అటుకులు—parboiled and husked paddy

uppu ఉప్పు—salt

kāramu కారము—chilly powder

chinthapandu చింతపండు—tamarind

kallu కల్లు—an intoxicating drink from the palm tree

sārāyi సారాయి—liquor

pāneeyamu పానీయము—drink

vindu విందు—dinner

āhvānamu ఆహ్వానము } —invitation
pilupu పిలుపు

House & Household articles

illu ఇల్లు—house, home

vākili వాకిలి—doorway

thalupu తలుపు—door

kitiki కిటికి—window

gōda గోడ—wall

punādi పునాది—foundation

gadapa గడప—threshold

doddi దొడ్డి—backyard

vasārā వసారా—varandah

āvaraṇa ఆవరణ—compound

padaka gadi పడక గది—bed-room

vanta illu వంట ఇల్లు—kitchen

bhōjanaśāla భోజనశాల—dining room

śāla శాల—hall

marugu doddi మరుగు దొడ్డి—closet

pogagottamu పొగగొట్టము—chimney

poyyi పొయ్యి } —hearth, oven
proyyi ప్రొయ్యి

snānapugadi స్నానపుగది—bath-room

mēda మేడ—a building with two or more storeys

bāvi బావి }—well
nooyi నూయి }—well

sthhambhamu స్థంభము—pillar

pusthakaSāla పుస్తకశాల—library-room

gadi గది—room

rāyi రాయి—stone

ituka ఇటుక—brick

penku పెంకు—tile

karra కఱ్ఱ—timber

isuka ఇసుక—sand

neeru నీరు—water

metlu మెట్లు—steps; staircase

anthasthhu అంతస్థు—storey

dābā డాబా—terrace

doolamu దూలము—beam

(pī) kappu (పై) కప్పు—roof; ceiling

pendebadda పెండెబద్ద—lath

mola మొల }—nail
mēku మేకు }—nail

cheela చీల—spike

gadiya గడియ—bolt

thālamu తాళము—lock

kappathālamu కప్పతాళము—padlock

balla బల్ల—bench, table

kurchee కుర్చీ—chair

madatha kurchee మడత కుర్చీ—folding chair

padaka kurchee పడక కుర్చీ—easy chair

manChamu మంచము—cot

pandiri పందిరి— cover for a cot or an open space

dōmothera దోమతెర—mosquito curtain

uyyela ఉయ్యాల—cradle

parupu పరుపు— bedding

prakka ప్రక్క—bed

d̄indu దిండు
thalagada తలగడ } —pillow

thalavīpu తలవైపు —head-end

kāḷḷavīpu కాళ్ళవైపు—foot-end

pette పెట్టె—box

visanakar̄r̄a విసనకఱ్ఱ—fan

ad̄d̄amu అద్దము—mirror

duvvena దువ్వెన—comb

bottu బొట్టు—(vermillion) mark (on the face)

kunkuma కుంకుమ—a red powder for *bottu*

suvāsanathīlamu సువాసనతైలము—scented oil

aththaru అత్తరు—scent

panneeru పన్నీరు—rose-water

agaruvaththi అగరువత్తి—scented stick

d̄hoopamu ధూపము—scented smoke

sāmbrāṇi సాంబ్రాణి—benzoin

d̄eepamu దీపము—light

vaththi వత్తి—wick

aggipulla అగ్గిపుల్ల—match stick

aggipette అగ్గిపెట్టె—match-box

patamu పటము—picture

kātuka కాటుక—collyrium

gand̄hamu గంధము
chand̄anamu చందనము } —sandalwood paste

kasthoori కస్తూరి—musk

punugu పునుగు
javād̄i జవాది } —civet

lakka లక్క—lac

chāpa చాప = mat

thivāchee తివాచి—carpet

bontha బొంత—quilt

beeruvā బీరువా—almirah

ginne గిన్నె—cup; vessel

pingān̄ee పింగాణీ—chinaware
garite గరిటె—ladle
chemchā చెంచా—spoon
sibbi సిబ్బి—metal cover
visthari విస్తరి—leafy plate for taking food
kanC̄hamu కంచేము—metal plate
chembu చెంబు—ewer
peeta పీట—wooden seat
bind̄e బిందె—water-container (metal)
kāgu కాగు—cauldron
kunda కుండ—pot
C̄hatti చేట్టి—cooking pot
muntha ముంత—small pot, mug
mookudu మూకుడు—pan
koojā కూజా—pitcher
jādi జాడి—jar
penamu పెనము—metal pan
dabbā డబ్బా—tin container
r̄āthichippa ఱాతిచిప్ప—stone-ware
pal̄l̄emu పళ్లెము—plate
r̄ōlu ఱోలు—mortar
r̄ōkali ఱోకలి—pestle
chēta చేట—winnow
jalleda జల్లెడ—sieve
cheepuru చీపురు—broom (stick)

panimuttu పనిముట్టు—instrument, tool

kaththipeeta కత్తిపీట—an instrument to chop or cut vegetables with

kaththi కత్తి—knife.

gampa గంప
thatta తట్ట } —basket

butta బుట్ట—small basket

sanchi సంచి—bag

chēthisanchi చేతిసంచి—hand bag

vantacher̄aku వంటచెఱకు
kattelu కట్టెలు } —fuel

boggu బొగ్గు—charcoal

pidukalu పిడుకలు—dung-cakes

mootha మూత—lid, cover

gāju sāmānulu గాజు సామానులు—glass-ware

seesā సీసా—bottle

biradā బిరడా—cork

mīnapuvaththi మైనపువత్తి—candle

kavvamu కవ్వము—churning stick

gottamu గొట్టము—tube

kaththera కత్తెర—scissors

garaatee గరాటీ—funnel

Dress & Relative Materials.

vasthramulu వస్త్రములు
d̄usthulu దుస్తులు } —clothes

d̄hōvathi ధోవతి—*dhotee* (lion-cloth)

uththareeyamu ఉత్తరీయము—upper cloth

c̄hokkā చొక్కా—shirt

jēbu జేబు—pocket

lāgu లాగు—pant

gundee గుండీ—button

thalapāga తలపాగ—head-dress

cheppulu చెప్పులు
pādarakshalu పాదరక్షలు } —shoes (chappals)

chēthigudda చేతిగుడ్డ—handkerchief

tōpee టోపీ—cap

r̄avike రవికె—blouse, jacket

cheera చీర—*saree* (a cloth worn by ladies)

jalathāru జలతారు—gold or silver lace

pattu పట్టు—silk

d̄ood̄i దూది
praththi ప్రత్తి } —cotton

*d*uppati దుప్పటి—bed-cover etc.

s̄āluva శాలువ—shawl

galeebu గలీబు—pillow-cover (దిండుముసుగు)

kambal̄i కంబళి
gongal̄i గొంగళి } —blanket

naga నగ—jewel

hāramu హారము—necklace

golusu గొలుసు—chain

ungaramu ఉంగరము—ring

kadiyamu కడియము—bracelet, or anklet

chevipōgulu చెవిపోగులు—ear-rings

*d̄id̄d*ulu దిద్దులు—ear-stars

gājulu గాజులు—bangles

varusa వరుస—row

Beasts, Birds & Reptiles

janthuvu జంతువు } —beast, animal
mrugamu మృగము }

āvu ఆవు—cow

ed̄d̄u ఎద్దు—ox

bar̄r̄e బఱ్ఱె } —she-buffalo
gēd̄e గేదె }

d̄ooda దూడ—calf

d̄unnapōthu దున్నపోతు—he-buffalo

gur̄r̄amu గుఱ్ఱము—horse

gādid̄a గాడిద—ass

kanc̄haragādid̄a కంచరగాడిద—mule

ēnugu ఏనుగు—elephant

onte ఒంటె—camel

nippukōdi నిప్పుకోడి—ostrich

kōthi కోతి—monkey

pilli పిల్లి—cat

kukka కుక్క—dog

pand̄i పంది—pig

adavipand̄i అడవిపంది—wild-boar

mundlapand̄i ముండ్లపంది—porcupine

elugubanṭi ఎలుగుబంటి—bear

puli పులి—tiger

chir̄uthapuli చిఱుతపులి—leopard

thōdēlu తోడేలు—wolf

simhamu సింహము—lion

kund̄ēlu కుందేలు—hare

nakka నక్క—jackal

guntanakka గుంటనక్క—fox

jinka జింక—deer

d̄uppi దుప్పి—male-deer

lēdi లేడి—stag

gor̄r̄e గొఱ్ఱె—sheep

mēka మేక—gcat

mand̄a మంద—herd

eluka ఎలుక—rat

chitteluka చిట్టెలుక—mouse

thonda తొండ
oosaravilli ఊసరవిల్లి } —chameleon

udutha ఉడుత—squirrel

mungisa ముంగిస—mongoose

kāki కాకి—crow

pic̄hchuka పిచ్చుక—sparrow

pāvuramu పావురము—pigeon

guvva గువ్వ—dove

grad̄d̄a గ్రద్ద—kite

dēga డేగ—hawk

rāband̄u రాబందు—vulture

konga కొంగ—crane

grudlagooba గ్రుడ్లగూబ—owl

chiluka చిలుక—parrot

kōkila కోకిల—cuckoo

hamsa హంస—swan

nemali నెమలి—peacock, peahen

kōdi కోడి—cock, hen

bāthu బాతు— goose, gander

pāmu పాము—snake

thrāchupāmu త్రాచుపాము—cobra

vishamu విషము—poison

thēlu తేలు—scorpion

balli బల్లి—lizard

sāleedu సాలీడు—spider

purugu పురుగు—worm

cheema చీమ—ant

chedalu చెదలు—white ant

nalli నల్లి—bug

dōma దోమ—mosquito

eega ఈగ—fly

kandireega కందిరీగ—wasp

thēneteega తేనెటీగ—bee

gongali purugu గొంగళి పురుగు—cater pillar

midutha మిడుత—locust

chēpa చేప—fish

mosali మొసలి—crocodile

thimingilamu తిమింగిలము—whale

sorachēpa సొరచేప—shark

polusu పొలుసు—fin

gabbilamu గబ్బిలము—bat

thondamu తొండము—trunk

thōka తోక—tail

danthamu దంతము—tusk

meesamulu మీసములు—whiskers

gitta గిట్ట—hoof

jalaga జలగ—leech

naththa నత్త—snail

thābēlu తాబేలు—tortoise

kappa కప్ప—frog

endrakāya ఎండ్రకాయ, peetha పీత —crab

Sounds of Animals, Birds, etc.

āvu "ambā" anunu ఆవు "అంబా" అనును

pilli "myâvu" ,, పిల్లి "మ్యావు" ,,

kukka mor̄ugunu కుక్క మొఱుగును

edd̄u r̄ankevēyunu ఎద్దు అంకెవేయును

gādid̄a ōndrapettunu గాడిద ఓండ్రపెట్టును

gur̄r̄amu sakilinchunu గుఱ్ఱము సకిలించును

kōthi kichakichalādunu కోతి కిచకిచలాడును

ēnugu gheemkarimchunu ఏనుగు ఘీంకరించును

pedd̄apuli gāndrinchunu పెద్దపులి గాండ్రించును

simhamu garjinchunu సింహము గర్జించును

kōdi "kokkorōkō" anunu కోడి "కొక్కొరోకో" అనును

pāmu busakottunu పాము బుసకొట్టును

kōkila "koo" ani kooyunu కోకిల "కూ" అనికూయును

Conveyances.

vāhanamu వాహనము—carriage, conveyance

vimānamu విమానము—aeroplane

pallaki పల్లకి }—palanquin
mēnā మేనా }

rathamu రథము—chariot

chakramu చక్రము—wheel

jeenu జీను—saddle

kal̄l̄emu కళ్లెము—reins

koradā కొరడా—whip

vanthena వంతెన—bridge

bandi బండి—cart

padava పడవ—boat

nouka నౌక—ship

kāluva కాలువ—canal

thoomu తూము—tunnel

Vegetables,

kooragāyalu కూరగాయలు—vegetables
vankāyalu వంకాయలు—brinjals
beer̄akāyalu బీఱకాయలు—angular gourds
chikkudukāyalu చిక్కుడుకాయలు—beans
gummadikāya గుమ్మడికాయ—pumpkin
rāmamulagakāya రామములగకాయ—tomato
velagakāya వెలగకాయ—wood-apple
d̄hōsakāya ధోసకాయ—cucumber
kākarakāya కాకరకాయ—bitter gourd
potlakāya పొట్లకాయ—snake-gourd
sorakāya సొరకాయ—bottle gourd
bendakāya బెండకాయ—lady's fingers
munagakāya మునగకాయ—drumstick
kōsupuvvu కోసుపువ్వు—cauliflower
thammakāya తమ్మకాయ—sword bean
aratikāya అరటికాయ—plantain
boodid̄agummadikāya బూడిదగుమ్మడికాయ—wax-gourd
chēmad̄umpa చేమదుంప—hayne
chilagadad̄umpa చిలగడదుంప
genusugadda గెనుసుగడ్డ } —sweat potato
mullangi ముల్లంగి—radish
d̄abbakāya దబ్బకాయ—citron
nimmakāya నిమ్మకాయ—lemon
chukkakoora చుక్కకూర—rumex
gōgukoora గోగుకూర—rossell, sorrel
menthikoora మెంతికూర—fenugreek
pachimirepakāyalu పచ్చిమిరెపకాయలు—green chillies

koththimiri కొత్తిమిరి—spinach

pandlu పండ్లు—fruit

māmidipandu మామిడిపండు—mango

nārinjapandu నారింజపండు—orange

panasapandu పనసపండు—jack fruit

dānimmapandu దానిమ్మపండు—pomegrenate

anāsapandu అనాసపండు—pine apple

jāmapandu జామపండు—guava

aratipandu అరటిపండు—plantain

kharjoorapupandlu ఖర్జూరపుపండ్లు—dates

kobbarikāya కొబ్బరికాయ—cocoanut

bādamukāya బాదముకాయ—almond

guththi గుత్తి—bunch

puppodi పుప్పొడి—pollen

kanche కంచె—hedge, fence

poda పొద—bush

theege తీగె—creeper

iguru ఇగురు
chiguru చిగురు } —tender leaf

marrichettu మర్రిచెట్టు—banyan tree

thummachettu తుమ్మచెట్టు—peepul tree

chinthachettu చింతచెట్టు—tamarind tree

vepachettu వేపచెట్టు—margosa tree

māmidichettu మామిడిచెట్టు—mango tree

thātichettu తాటిచెట్టు—palmyra tree

kobbarichettu కొబ్బరిచెట్టు—cocoanut tree

cheraku చెఱకు—sugar-cane

praththichettu ప్రత్తిచెట్టు—cotton plant

ginja గింజ—seed

molaka మొలక—seedling

mokka మొక్క—plant

chettu చెట్టు—tree

komma కొమ్మ—branch

vēru వేరు—root

kāndamu కాండము—trunk

mogga మొగ్గ—bud

āku ఆకు—leaf

poovu పూవు—flower

kāya కాయ—raw fruit

thodima తొడిమ—stem

beradu బెరడు—bark

rēku రేకు—petal

rasamu రసము—juice

Government.

prajalu ప్రజలు
janulu జనులు } —people

janasankhya జనసంఖ్య—population

grāmeen̄ulu గ్రామీణులు—village folk

nāgarikulu నాగరికులు—citizens

jāthi జాతి—nation

jātheeyatha జాతీయత—nationality

varn̄amu వర్ణము
kulamu కులము } —caste

mathamu మతము—religion

rājyamu రాజ్యము—kingdom

d̄ēS̄amu దేశము—country

khandamu ఖండము—continent

ella ఎల్ల—boundary

ennikalu ఎన్నికలు—elections

niyāmakamu నియామకము—appointment

ērpātu ఏర్పాటు—arrangement

rāyabāri రాయబారి—ambassador

vargamu వర్గము—group, class

mandalamu మండలము—district

rājad̄hāni రాజధాని—presidency, capital (city)

ad̄hyakshudu అధ్యక్షుడు—president; chairman

upād̄hyakshudu ఉపాధ్యక్షుడు—vice president; vice-chairman.

kāryad̄arS̄i కార్యదర్శి—secretary

sahāyakāryad̄arS̄i సహాయకార్యదర్శి—Assistant Secretary

samyukthakāryad̄arS̄i సంయుక్తకార్యదర్శి—joint secretary.

sabhyudu సభ్యుడు—member

gouravasabhyudu గౌరవసభ్యుడు—honorary **member**

sabha సభ—council, meeting

Sāsanasabha శాసనసభ-parliament, legislative **assembly**

rājyāngamu రాజ్యాంగము—constitution

chattamu చేట్టము
Sāsanamu శాసనము } —act

nibandhanalu నిబంధనలు—regulations

niyamamulu నియమములు—rules

upanibandhanalu ఉపనిబంధనలు—bye-laws

theermānamu తీర్మానము—resolution

āya-vyaya-pattika ఆయవ్యయపట్టిక—budget

anchanā అంచనా—estimate

sammathi సమ్మతి—vote; agreement

pannu పన్ను—tax

Sisthu శిస్తు—land-tax

mujarā ముజరా—refund

vārtha వార్త—news

vārthapathrika వార్తపత్రిక—newspaper

rāju రాజు—king

rāni రాణి—queen

yuvarāju యువరాజు—prince

manthri మంత్రి—**minister**

kēndrama కేంద్రము—**centre**

sthhānikamu స్థానికము—**local**

rājakumārudu రాజకుమారుడు—**king's son, prince**

rājakumāri రాజకుమారి—princess, king's daughter

chakravarthi చక్రవర్తి—emperor

simhāsananu సింహాసనము—throne

pattābhishēkamu పట్టాభిషేకము—coronation

Vocations & Professions

vyavasāyamu వ్యవసాయము—agriculture

nāgali నాగలి—plough

rīthu రైతు
vyavasāyadārudu వ్యవసాయదారుడు } —cultivator, farmer

bhooswāmi భూస్వామి—land-lord

koulu కౌలు—lease

kouludārudu కౌలుదారుడు—tenant

bāduga బాడుగ—rent

vyāpāramu వ్యాపారము—business

varthakamu వర్తకము—trade

varthakudu వర్తకుడు—merchant

dukāṇamu దుకాణము
angadi అంగడి } —shop

angadiveedhi అంగడివీధి—bazar

thōta తోట—garden

thōtapani తోటపని—gardening

chēnu చేను
polamu పొలము } —field, land

gattu గట్టు—bund

kuppa కుప్ప—heap, stack

panta పంట—harvest

thoonika తూనిక—weight

kolatha కొలత—measure

kolathabadda కొలతబద్ద—measure stick

(sari) haddu (సరి) హద్దు—boundary

meṛaka మెఱక—high level

meṛakachēnu మెఱకచేను—dry-land

kādi కాడి—yoke

goddali గొడ్డలి—axe

gaddapāra గడ్డపార
gunapamu గునపము } —crow-bar

kodavali కొడవలి—sickle

eruvu ఎరువు—manure

kanche కంచె—fence

bātu బాటు—weight

gajamu గజము—yard

nēla నేల
matti మట్టి } —earth

kanki కంకి—ear of corn

kalupu కలుపు—weeds

sāramu సారము—fertility

gāde గాదె—barn

sāgu సాగు—cultivation

beedu బీడు—waste land

kallamu కల్లము—thrashing floor

pachchika పచ్చిక—grass, pasture

pachchika bayalu పచ్చికబయలు—meadow

pallamu పల్లము—low level

saruku సరుకు—merchandise

pallapuchēnu పల్లపుచేను—wet land

rokkamu రొక్కము—cash

dhānyamu ధాన్యము—paddy, grain

appu అప్పు
aruvu అరువు } —loan

theege thrāsu తీగె త్రాసు—spring balance

thrāsu త్రాసు
thakkeda తక్కెడ } —balance

katta కట్ట—bale, bundle

varusa వరుస—row

mullu ముల్లు—pointer

asalu అసలు—principal

dande దండె—beam of a balance

vaddi వడ్డి—interest

niluva నిలువ—balance (of stock etc.)

kāthā కాతా—ledger

lekka లెక్క—sum, account

chitthā చిఠా—journal

paddu పద్దు—entry

nagadu chitthā నగదు చిఠా—cash book

bāruvaddi బారువడ్డి—simple interest

chakravaddi చక్రవడ్డి—compound interest

dhara ధర—rate

vela వెల—price

giddangi గిడ్డంగి—store house

vasthuvu వస్తువు—article

sēvakudu సేవకుడు—servant

gumāsthā గుమాస్తా—clerk

bānisa బానిస—slave

yajamāni యజమాని—master

sanchi సంచి—bag

panivādu పనివాడు—workman

ādāyamu ఆదాయము
rābadi రాబడి } —income

vyayamu వ్యయము—expenditure

lābhamu లాభము—profit

nashtamu నష్టము—loss

krayamu క్రయము—purchase

vikrayamu విక్రయము—sale

mārakamu మారకము—exchange

d̄ravyamu ద్రవ్యము—money

nān̄emu నాణెము—coin

mād̄iri మాదిరి—sample

egumathi ఎగుమతి—export

digumathi దిగుమతి—import

run̄amu ఋణము }
appu అప్పు } —loan

run̄ad̄ātha ఋణదాత—creditor

run̄asthhudu ఋణస్థుడు }
bākeed̄ārudu బాకీదారుడు } —debtor

bēramu బేరము—bargain

patti పట్టి—invoice

pettubadi పెట్టుబడి—investment, capital

bhāgamu భాగము—part

bhāgasthhudu భాగస్థుడు—partner

thākattu తాకట్టు—mortgage

pathramu పత్రము— bond

chellu చెల్లు—**re-payment**

jama జమ—**credit**

kharchu ఖర్చు—**debit**

pēchchu పెచ్చు—**excess**

thachchu తచ్చు }
tharugu తఱుగు } —deficit

tōku టోకు—wholesale

chillara చిల్లర—retail

uththaramu ఉత్తరము—letter

vidud̄ala విడుదల—release

āsthi ఆస్తి—asset

appu అప్పు—liability

sthhirāsthi స్థిరాస్తి—immovable property

charāsthi చరాస్తి—moveable property

prakatana ప్రకటన—advertisement

bayānā బయానా—advance

darjeevādu దర్జీవాడు—tailor
chākali చాకలి—washerman
mangali మంగలి—barber
chithrakārudu చిత్రకారుడు—painter
vīdyudu వైద్యుడు—doctor
nyāyavādi న్యాయవాది—lawyer
jyōthishkudu జ్యోతిష్కుడు—astronomer
kavi కవి—poet
vadrangi వడ్రంగి—carpenter
silpi శిల్పి—architect
thāpee panivādu తాపీ పనివాడు—mason
vantavādu వంటవాడు—cook (male)
vantalakka వంటలక్క—cook (female)
kasāyivādu కసాయివాడు—butcher
pallevādu పల్లెవాడు—fisherman
thōtamāli తోటమాలి—gardener
vētakādu వేటకాడు }—hunter
bōyavādu బోయవాడు }—hunter
gollavādu గొల్లవాడు—shepherd
pātakādu పాటకాడు—songster
pātakaththe పాటకత్తె—songstress
panikaththe పనికత్తె—servant-maid
ātakādu ఆటకాడు—player
natakudu నటకుడు—actor
nati నటి—actress
thelakavādu తెలకవాడు—oilman
kamsāli కంసాలి—goldsmith
thagarapu panivādu తగరపు పనివాడు—tinman

raSeedu రశీదు—receipt
jābithā జాబితా—list
vruththi వృత్తి—profession
addakamu అద్దకము—dyeing
aChchu అచ్చు—print
kammari కమ్మరి—blacksmith
kanChari కంచరి—brass founder
sālevādu సాలెవాడు—weaver
gāradivādu గారడివాడు—juggler
hāsyagādu హాస్యగాడు—buffoon
upāDhyāyudu ఉపాధ్యాయుడు—teacher

suththi సుత్తి—hammer
Dimma దిమ్మ—anwil
kolimi కొలిమి—furnace
padugu పడుగు—warp
pēka పేక—woof
thrādu త్రాడు—rope
maggamu మగ్గము—loom
nāde నాడె, kande కండె—shuttle
vala వల—net
era ఎర—prey

kachēri కచేరి, kāryālayamu కార్యాలయము—office
karmāgāramu కర్మాగారము—workshop
yanthramu యంత్రము—machine
yanthrāgāramu యంత్రాగారము—factory
jeethamu జీతము—salary, wages
badi బడి, pāttaSāla పాఠశాల—school
panthulu పంతులు—teacher
viDyārthhi విద్యార్థి—student (male)
viDyārthhini విద్యార్థిని—student (female)

pusthakamu పుస్తకము—book
kāgithamu కాగితము—paper
palaka పలక—slate
balapamu బలపము—slate-pencil
kalamu కలము—pen
selavu సెలవు—holiday

pātthamu పాఠము—lesson
aDhyāyamu అధ్యాయము—chapter
puta పుట—page
pankthi పంక్తి—line
gaDyamu గద్యము—prose
paDyamu పద్యము—poetry

anuvādamu అనువాదము—translation
vid̄yārthhi vēthanamu విద్యార్థి వేతనము—scholarship
seemasunnapu mukka సీమసున్నపు ముక్క—chalk piece
moolamu మూలము—text
arthhamu అర్థము—meaning
thāthparyamu తాత్పర్యము—summary
vyākhyānamu వ్యాఖ్యానము—commentary
nallaballa నల్లబల్ల—black board
charithra చరిత్ర—history
bhoogōlaśāsthramu భూగోళశాస్త్రము—geography
khagōlaśāsthramu ఖగోళశాస్త్రము—astronomy
lekkalu లెక్కలు—mathematics
ankagaṇithamu అంకగణితము—arthmetic
ankamu అంకము—act (of a drama)
anuband̄hamu అనుబంధము—appendix
sankhya సంఖ్య } —number
anke అంకె }
bhāgamu భాగము—part
moththamu మొత్తము—total
koodika కూడిక—addition
theesivētha తీసివేత—subtraction
hechchavētha హెచ్చవేత—multiplication
bhāgahāramu భాగహారము—division
samānamu సమానము—equal
chiththu చిత్తు—rough (draft)
śud̄d̄haprathi శుద్ధప్రతి—fair copy
beejagaṇithamu బీజగణితము—Algebra
rēkhāgaṇithamu రేఖాగణితము—geometry

neethiS̄āsthramu నీతిశాస్త్రము—ethics

prakruthiS̄asthramu ప్రకృతిశాస్త్రము—natural science

vignānaS̄asthramu విజ్ఞానశాస్త్రము—science

prāthamikavid̄ya ప్రాథమికవిద్య—elementary education

unnathavid̄ya ఉన్నతవిద్య—higher education

vayŌjana vid̄ya వయోజన విద్య—adult education

pareeksha పరీక్ష—examination

praS̄napathramu ప్రశ్నపత్రము—question paper

praS̄na ప్రశ్న—question

samād̄hānamu సమాధానము }—answer
javābu జవాబు }

upŌd̄ghāthamu ఉపోద్ఘాతము—preface

vishayasoochika విషయసూచిక—index

thappu తప్పు—error

oppu ఒప్పు—correctness

kal̄a కళ—art

kal̄aS̄āla కళాశాల—college

patamu పటము—map, picture

sangeethamu సంగీతము—music

nātakamu నాటకము—drama

rangamu రంగము—scene

Some Useful Adjectives

manchi మంచి—good
chedu చెడు—bad
potti పొట్టి—short
podugu పొడుగు—long
lāvagu లావగు—opulent
sannani సన్నని—lean
d̄aḹasari దళసరి } —thick
d̄attamagu దట్టమగు }
and̄amīna అందమైన—beautiful
and̄aviheenamīna అందవిహీనమైన—ugly
thiyyani తియ్యని—sweet
pullani పుల్లని—sour
chēd̄īna చేదైన—bitter
nindu నిండు—full
vatti వట్టి—empty
uppani ఉప్పని—of a saltish taste
kārapu కారపు—of a pungent taste
suvāsanagala సువాసనగల—of a good smell
d̄urvāsanagala దుర్వాసనగల—of a bad smell
d̄oorapu దూరపు—distant
d̄aggaṟi దగ్గఱి—near
meththani మెత్తని—soft
gaṟukīna గఱుకైన—rough
c̄hallani చల్లని—cold
vēdi వేడి—hot
sunnithamīna సున్నితమైన—delicate
gatti గట్టి—hard

eththīna ఎత్తైన—high
lōthugānunna లోతుగానున్న—low
viŝālamagu విశాలమగు—spacious
iṟukagu ఇఱుకగు—congested
thelivigala తెలివిగల—clever
thelivilēni తెలివిలేని—stupid
vid̄ēŝee విదేశీ—foreign
swad̄ēŝee స్వదేశీ—indigenous
viluvagala విలువగల—valuable
velalēni వెలలేని—invaluable
beed̄a బీద } —poor
pēd̄a పేద }

bhāgyamugala భాగ్యముగల—rich

thellani తెల్లని—white

nallani నల్లని—black

er̄r̄ani ఎఱ్ఱని—red

pasupu pac̆hchani పసుపు పచ్చని—yellow

āku pac̆hchani ఆకు పచ్చని—green

neeli నీలి—blue

ood̄ā ఊదా—violet

chithravarn̄amugala చిత్రవర్ణముగల—multicoloured

r̄āthi ఱాతి— made of stone

bangārapu బంగారపు— ,, gold

vendi వెండి— ,, silver

inupa ఇనుప— ,, iron

iththadi ఇత్తడి— ,, brass

rāgi రాగి— ,, copper

kanchu కంచు— ,, bronze

thagarapu తగరపు— ,, tin

d̄anthapu దంతపు— ,, ivory

koyya కొయ్య— ,, wood

kāgithapu కాగితపు— ,, paper

ārthhika ఆర్థిక—financial

sāmud̄āyika సాముదాయిక—communal

sāmājika సామాజిక—social

Ihika ఐహిక—wordly

pāraloukika పారలౌకిక—of the other world

bhouthika భౌతిక—physical

thinnani తిన్నని—straight

yŏgyamagu యోగ్యమగు
arhathagala అర్హతగల
arhamagu అర్హమగు
thagina తగిన
} —fit, matching

C̄hāla చాల
ekkuva ఎక్కువ
} —much

anni అన్ని—all (number) ā ఆ—that, those

antha అంత—all (quantity) ee ఈ—this, those

kontha కొంత—some (")

konni కొన్ని— ,, (number)

inni ఇన్ని—so many

intha ఇంత—so much

entha ఎంత—how much

enni ఎన్ని—how many

sukhamagu సుఖమగు—happy

kashtamagu కష్టమగు—difficult

kolad̄i కొలది
kod̄d̄i కొద్ది
konchemu కొంచెము
} —a little, few

Some useful Adverbs etc.

thvaragā త్వరగా
thond̄aragā తొందరగా
vadigā వడిగా
} —swiftly

mellagā మెల్లగా—gently

d̄ooramugā దూరముగా— distantly

d̄aggar̄agā దగ్గరగా—near (ly)
meththagā మెత్తగా—softly
gattigā గట్టిగా—hard (ly)
and̄amugā అందముగా—beautifully
asahyamugā అసహ్యముగా—ugly
parasparamu పరస్పరము—mutually
ēkagreevamugā ఏకగ్రీవముగా—unanimously
thiyyagā తియ్యగా—sweetly
pullagā పుల్లగా—sourly
chēd̄ugā చేదుగా—bitterly
c̄hallagā చల్లగా—coolly
vec̄hchagā వెచ్చగా—warmly
vēdigā వేడిగా—hot
thellagā తెల్లగా—white
nallagā నల్లగా—black
mund̄ugā ముందుగా—before
venukagā వెనుకగా—behind
vad̄ulugā వదులుగా—loose (ly)
biguthugā బిగుతుగా—tightly
thappaka తప్పక—without fail
ālasyamugā ఆలస్యముగా—with delay
pend̄alakada పెందలకడ—early
eppudunu ఎప్పుడును—always
ventanē వెంటనే—immediately
prasthuthamu ప్రస్తుతము—for the time being

adiyunugāka అదియునుగాక—further, not only that

marala మరల—again

mariyu (nu) మరియు (ను)—and

thappa తప్ప
kāka కాక } —except

tharāchugā తఱచుగా—frequently

aruḍugā అరుదుగా—rarely

mikkili మిక్కిలి
ekkuva ఎక్కువ } —very, greatly

appudē అప్పుడే
idivarakē ఇదివరకే } —already

dādāpu దాదాపు
sumāru సుమారు
ramārami రమారమి } —almost

appudu అప్పుడు—then

ippudu ఇప్పుడు—now

eppudu ఎప్పుడు—when

akkada అక్కడ—there

ikkada ఇక్కడ—here

ekkada ఎక్కడ—where

enduku ఎందుకు—why

etlu ఎట్లు—how

itlu ఇట్లు—in this way

atlu అట్లు—in that way

chālunu చాలును—enough

ani అని—that (subordinative conjunction of introduction)

poorvamu పూర్వము—once upon a time

eḍurugā ఎదురుగా—in front of

* yu యు, nu ను, kooda కూడ—also

tharuvātha తరువాత
anthata అంతట
pimmata పిమ్మట
atupimmata ఆటుపిమ్మట } —after (wards)

iteevala ఇటీవల—recently

mellagā మెల్లగా—slowly

edathegaka ఎడతెగక
viduvakunda విడువకుండ } —incessantly

māti mātiki మాటి మాటికి—repeatedly

nu ను is added to nouns or pronouns ending in u.
yu యు is added to nouns or pronouns ending in
letters other than u.

sukhamugā సుఖముగా—happily

kashtamugā కష్టముగా—with difficulty

krinḍata క్రిందట—before, back, ago

sarigā సరిగా—exactly, correctly

ounu ఔను—yes

kāḍu కాదు—no

lēḍu లేదు—not

kāni కాని—but

ēla ఏల—why

ēni ఏని—if

inkanu ఇంకను—still, yet

ayinanu అయినను
ayinappatikini అయినప్పటికిని } —though, even if, never the less, even then

ooraka ఊరక, or oorakanē ఊరకనే—simply—without anything particular

etlayinanu ఎట్లయినను—however

lēka లేక } — or
kāni కాని } — but

kanuka కనుక
kābatti కాబట్టి } —therefore

enā ఏనా—interrogative termination added to a noun or pronoun

ayinachō అయినచో
ayinayedala అయినయెడల } —if

enḍukanagā ఎందుకనగా
ēlana ఏలన } —because

ēmōyani ఏమోయని—lest

āhā ఆహా! ōhō ఓహో!	—interjection expressing wonder	
hā హా hathavidhee హతవిధీ	,, ,,	sorrow
mēlu మేలు mēlu mēlu మేలు మేలు	,, ,,	approval or admiration
kadā కద (gada గద) kadā కదా (gadā గదా) kādā కాదా (gādā గాదా)	-(confirmatory interjection)	

Some useful (Verbal) Roots

čhoočhu చూచు—see (to*see)

vinu విను—hear

thinu తిను—eat

thrāgu త్రాగు—drink

mringu మ్రింగు—swallow

vāsanačhoočhu వాసనచూచు—smell

ruchičhoočhu రుచిచూచు—taste

mātalādu మాటలాడు—talk

vāgu వాగు—chatter

ālōčhinčhu ఆలోచించు—think

niščhayinčhu నిశ్చయించు—settle, decide

angeekarinčhu అంగీకరించు—agree

vichārinčhu విచారించు—feel sorry, enquire

duhkhinčhu దుఃఖించు—cry

ēdchu ఏడ్చు—cry aloud

navvu నవ్వు—laugh

---

* add "to" before every meaning.

pâḍu పాడు—sing

ādu ఆడు—dance, play

cheppu చెప్పు—tell

anu అను—say

anukonu అనుకొను—think

peelchu పీల్చు—breathe in

thittu తిట్టు—insult

kottu కొట్టు—beat

poojinChu పూజించు—worship

vrāyu వ్రాయు—write

Chaduvu చదువు—read

vallinChu వల్లించు—recite

thiraskarinChu తిరస్కరించు—refuse, oppose

edurchu ఎదుర్చు—oppose

deevinChu దీవించు } —bless
āSeervadinChu ఆశీర్వదించు }

prārththinChu ప్రార్థించు—pray

brathimālu బ్రతిమాలు—request, implore

samthrupthiparaChu సంతృప్తిపరచు—satisfy

ēdipinChu ఏడిపించు—to make one cry

thrupthipadu తృప్తిపడు—to be satisfled

gouravinChu గౌరవించు—honour

sukhapadu సుఖపడు—to be happy

sukhaparaChu సుఖపరచు—to make one happy

oopiri viduChu ఊపిరి విడుచు—breathe out

viduChu విడుచు } —release, omit
vadalu వదలు }

paṭṭukonu పట్టుకొను—catch

ekku ఎక్కు—climb up

digu దిగు—climb dowh

koorchundu కూర్చుండు—sit

niluChundu నిలుచుండు—stand

lepu లేపు—rouse

pandukonu పండుకొను—lie down

nidrapŌvu నిద్రపోవు
nidrinchu నిద్రించు } —to sleep

gurakapettu గుఱకపెట్టు—snore

kadalu కదలు—move

nadachu నడచు
naduchu నడుచు } —walk

parugeththu పరుగెత్తు—run

padu పడు—fall

padavēyu పడవేయు— to fell

lēchu లేచు—rise up

kadalakunda కదలకుండు—to be steady

vangu వంగు—stoop, bend (intransitive)

vanchu వంచు—to bend (transitive)

mŌyu మోయు—carry

ichchu ఇచ్చు—give

theesikonu తీసికొను—take

appichchu అప్పిచ్చు—lend

appu theerchu అప్పు తీర్చు—repay

konu కొను—buy

ammu అమ్ము—sell

dinchu దించు—bring down

eththukonu ఎత్తుకొను—take up

piluchu పిలుచు—call

kŌpapadu కోపపడు—chide

bedirinchu బెదిరించు—threaten

kshaminchu క్షమించు—forgive

Ōdārchu ఓదార్చు—console

kŌru కోరు—wish

biginchu బిగించు—tighten

vadalucheyu వదలుచేయు—loose

thirigi vachchu తిరిగి వచ్చు—to return (to come back)

thirigi ichchu తిరిగి ఇచ్చు—to return (something)

danchu దంచు
nooru నూరు } —to pound (rice etc)

thrippu త్రిప్పు—to turn (something)

thirugu తిరుగు—wander, turn round;

prayanamucheyu ప్రయాణముచేయు—travel

pŌvu పోవు—go

vachchu వచ్చు—come

pondu పొందు—obtain

thechchu తెచ్చు—get

theesikonivachu తీసికొనివచ్చు—bring

pāducheēyu పాడుచేయు—spoil

bāguchēyu బాగుచేయు—repair

mōsaginchu మోసగించు—deceive

nammu నమ్ము—believe

namminchu నమ్మించు—make one believe

(pra) yathninchu (ప్ర) యత్నించు—try

sādhinchu సాధించు—achieve

geluchu గెలుచు—win

ōdu ఓడు—be defeated

ōdinchu ఓడించు—defeat

kalupu కలుపు—mix, join, add

vidadeeyu విడదీయు—separate

visuru విసురు—grind

bhāginchu భాగించు—divide

koodu కూడు—add

theesivēyu తీసివేయు—subtract

hechchavēyu హెచ్చవేయు—multiply

naSimpajēyu నశింపజేయు—destroy

puttinchu పుట్టించు—create

penchu పెంచు—grow

pōshinchu పోషించు—maintain, tend

lekkinčhu లెక్కించు—count

veḋaku వెదకు—search

kanugonu కనుగొను—find

thelisikonu తెలిసికొను—know

vivarinčhu వివరించు—explain

thelupu తెలుపు
theliyabarachu తెలియబరచు } —to let one know

kattu కట్టు—bind, tie, build

mudivēyu ముడివేయు—tie

vippu విప్పు—loosen

thōlu తోలు—drive

mēpu మేపు—graze (causative)

mēyu మేయు—graze

mečhčhukonu మెచ్చుకొను—admire

adugu అడుగు
prašninčhu ప్రశ్నించు } —ask

yāchinčhu యాచించు—beg

sahāyapadu సహాయపడు—help

kaṟachu కఱచు—bite

pagulagottu పగులగొట్టు—break

mandu మండు—burn

vandu వండు—cook

udikinčhu ఉడికించు—to boil

eguru ఎగురు—fly, jump

kOyu కోయు
tharugu తఱుగు } —cut

āgu ఆగు—stop

mod̄alupettu మొదలుపెట్టు
prārambhinC̄hu ప్రారంభించు } —begin

poorthichēyu పూర్తిచేయు—finish

angeekarinC̄hu అంగీకరించు
oppukonu ఒప్పుకొను } —agree

nirākarinC̄hu నిరాకరించు—deny

bayaludēru బయలుదేరు—start

chēru చేరు—reach

vrēlādu వ్రేలాడు—hang

visiginC̄hu విసిగించు—vex

panichēyu పనిచేయు—work, serve

sid̄hd̄hamuchēyu సిద్ధముచేయు—prepare

ērpātuchēyu ఏర్పాటుచేయు—arrange

svārichēyu స్వారిచేయు—ride

prakāS̄inC̄hu ప్రకాశించు—shine

ud̄ayinC̄hu ఉదయించు—rise (as the sun)

asthaminC̄hu అస్తమించు—set

rakshinC̄hu రక్షించు
kāpādu కాపాడు } —save

pōgottukonu పోగొట్టుకొను—lose

ērikonu ఏరికొను—select, pick up

thongiC̄hooC̄hu తొంగిచూచు—peep

mud̄d̄u pettukonu ముద్దు పెట్టుకొను—kiss

kougalinc̄hu కౌగలించు—embrace

chēyu చేయు—do, make

nērpu నేర్పు—teach

nērchukonu నేర్చుకొను—learn

d̄umuku దుముకు—leap

ganthuluvēyu గంతులువేయు—jump

ac̄hc̄huvēyu అచ్చువేయు } —print
mud̄rinc̄hu ముద్రించు }

muttukonu ముట్టుకొను—touch

oopu ఊపు—swing

añac̄hu అణచు—suppress

d̄āgu దాగు—hide (oneself)

d̄āc̄hu దాచు—hide (a thing)

sñānamuchēyu స్నానముచేయు—bathe

eed̄u ఈదు—swim

agu అగు—become

undu ఉండు—be, stay

pāravēyu పారవేయుthrow

prōguchēyu ప్రోగుచేయు—gather

d̄ātu దాటు—cross

c̄hoopu చూపు—show

lāgu లాగు—pull

thrōyu త్రోయు—push

C̄huttaC̄huttu చుట్టచుట్టు—roll

kuttu కుట్టు—sew, sting

ooḥịnchu ఊహించు—imagine

gorugu గొరుగు—shave

gruchc̣hu గ్రుచ్చు—prick

pettu పెట్టు—put

koluC̄hu కొలుచు—measure

thooC̄hu తూచు—weigh

jāru జారు—slip

pāthu పాతు—bury

thravvu త్రవ్వు – dig

geeẏu గీయు—draw

moọyu మూయు—cover

māru మారు—change (intransitive)

mārchu మార్చు—change (transitive)

mānchu మాన్చు—cure

ālasyamuchēyu ఆలస్యముచేయు—delay

pāru పారు } —flow
pravahinC̄hu ప్రవహించు }

brathuku బ్రతుకు—live

C̄haC̄hC̄hu చచ్చు—die

pogaḍu పొగడు—praise

prēminC̄hu ప్రేమించు—love

nāku నాకు—lick

LETTER-WRITING

Application for a clerk's post

Sree Dhanam & Company Managerugāriki
శ్రీ ధనం అండ్ కంపెనీ మేనేజరుగారికి—

Sikındrābad̄u
సికింద్రాబాదు

Date 5-8-1951

P. Sivachand̄rayya vr^{ā}sukonna arjee
పి. శివచంద్రయ్య వ్రాసుకొన్న అర్జీ—

ayya,
అయ్యా,

thama kampeneelō konni gum^{ā}sthā pad̄avulu kh^{ā}leegā
తమ కంపెనీలో కొన్ని గుమస్తా పదవులు ఖాళీగా

unnavani thelisi, vānilō oka d̄ānikī nēnu ee ārjeeni
ఉన్నవని తెలిసి. వానిలో ఒక దానికై నేను ఈ అర్జీని

pampukonu chunn^{ā}nu.
పంపుకొను చున్నాను.

nēnu matriculation varakunu chaduvu konnānu Urdu,
నేను మెట్రిక్యులేషను వరకును చదువు కొన్నాను ఉర్దూ,

Telugu, English, bh^{ā}shalalō b^{ā}gug^{ā} vrāyagalanu, m^{ā}ta-
తెలుగు, ఇంగ్లీషు భాషలలో బాగుగా వ్రాయగలను మాట

l^{ā}dagalanu. Hindeelō kooda kontha pravēSamu kaladu.
లాడగలను. హిందీలో కూడ కొంత ప్రవేశము కలదు.

lōgada nēnu mā grāmamagu Annampoodilōni Sree Pīsā
లోగడ నేను మా గ్రామమగు అన్నంపూడిలోని శ్రీ పైసా

& Cō., lō gumāsthāga moodu samvathsaramulu panichēsi
అండ్ కో.,లో గుమాస్తాగా మూడు సంవత్సరములు పనిచేసి

yuntini anduchē nāku varthaka vyavahāramulalō manchi
యుంటిని. అందుచే నాకు వర్తక వ్యవహారములలో మంచి

parichayamu kaladu. vāru ichchina yōgyathā pathramunu
పరిచయము కలదు. వారు ఇచ్చిన యోగ్యతా పత్రమును

deeniventapampukonuchunnānu.nāvayassuiruvadiyēndlu
దీని వెంట పంపుకొనుచున్నాను. నావయస్సు ఇరువది యేండ్లు.

nāku thama kampeneelō gumāsthā pani dayachēyinchi
నాకు తమ కంపెనీలో గుమాస్తా పని దయచేయించి

nachō thrupthikaramugā panichēyagalanu.
నచో తృప్తికరముగా పనిచేయగలను.

chiththagimpavalenu,
చిత్తగింపవలెను,

thama vidhēyudu,
తమ విధేయుడు,

P. Sivachandrayya.
పి. శివచంద్రయ్య.

nā chirunāmā
నా చిరునామా :—

C/o. J. Gaṇapathi,
C/o. జె. గణపతి.
Bhāskara Villa
భాస్కర విల్లా
sikindrābādu
సికింద్రాబాదు

(Summary of the body of the letter)

Having come to understand that there are some vacancies of clerical posts in your company, I am applying for one of them.

I have studied upto matriculation and I can read and write well in Urdu, Telugu and English languages. I know Hindi also to some extent.

I worked for three years as a clark in M/s. Pisa & Co. at my native place, Annampoodi. I enclose the testimonial given by them to me.

I can work satisfactorily if you be pleased to favour me with a clerk's post in your company.

Leave Application

Sree Dhanam & Co. Manager gāriki — Sikindrābādu
శ్రీ ధనం అండ్ కొ. మేనేజరు గారికి— సికింద్రాబాదు

ayyā! — D. 5-9-1952.
అయ్యా!

rēpu nā kumāruni vivahamu erpātu chēyabadinan-
రేపు నా కుమారుని వివాహము ఏర్పాటు చేయబడినం

duna, dayachēsi nāku nēdu, rēpu, selavu ippincha gōru
దున, దయచేసి నాకు నేడు, రేపు, సెలవు ఇప్పించే గోరు

chunnānu.
చేన్నాను.

chiththagimpavalenu,
చిత్తగింపవలెను.

J. Venkōbā Rāo, gumas hā.
జె. వెంకోబా రావు, గుమస్తా,

Summary

As my son's marriage is fixed up for tomorrow, I request you to be kind enough to grant me leave for today and tomorrow.

A father's Letter to His son

Chi. Rāmuluku—āSeervachanamulu Rāmavaram
చి. రాములుకు ఆశీర్వచనములు రామవరం

D. 8–9–1952.

ikkada mēmu andaramunu kshēmamugā unnāmu.
ఇక్కడ మేము అందఱము క్షేమముగా ఉన్నాము.

—we are all safe here.

neevu akkada kshēmamugā unnāvani thalathunu.
నీవు అక్కడ క్షేమముగా ఉన్నావని తలతును.

—I hope you are doing well there.

neevadda nundi uththaramu vachchi nela dātinadi.
నీవద్ద నుండి ఉత్తరము వచ్చి నెల దాటినది.

—It is past one month since (the last) letter is received from you.

kaneesamu nelaku okasāri ayinanu neevu thappaka
కనీసము నెలకు ఒకసారి అయినను నీవు తప్పక

jābulu vrāyuChundavalenu.
జాబులు వ్రాయుచుండవలెను.

—you should be writing letters at least once in a month without fail.

SHORT STORIES

cheema--pāvuramu

చీమ—పావురము

The Ant and the Pigeon

oka chettu meeda oka pāvuramu nivasinchuchundenu
ఒక చెట్టు మీద ఒక పావురము నివసించుచుండెను.

—A pigeon was living on a tree

ā chettukrinda unna puttalō oka cheema nivasinchu
ఆ చెట్టుక్రింద ఉన్న పుట్టలో ఒక చీమ నివసించు

chundenu.
చుండెను.

—An ant was living in an ant-hill which was under the tree.

avi rendunu mikkili snēhamu kaligi yundenu.
అవి రెండును మిక్కిలి స్నేహము కలిగి యుండెను.

—They both were very friendly (with each other)

okanādu ā cheema chettu prakkana unna cheruvulō
ఒకనాడు ఆ చీమ చెట్టు ప్రక్కన ఉన్న చెఱువులో

padenu.
పడెను.

—one day the ant fell into the tank beside the tree.

adi pāvuramu choochenu.
అది పావురము చూచెను.

—the pigeon saw it

adi ventanē oka ākunu neetilō cheema d̄aggar̄agā
అది వెంటనే ఒక ఆకును నీటిలో చీమ దగ్గఱగా

padavēsenu.
పడవేసెను.

—it threw a leaf immediately into the water near the ant.

cheema ā ākunu pattukoni d̄āni meed̄iki ekkenu.
చీమ ఆ ఆకును పట్టుకొని దాని మీదికి ఎక్కెను.

—the ant caught hold of the leaf and climbed upon it.

ā āku gāliki nemmad̄igā odduku chērenu.
ఆ ఆకు గాలికి నెమ్మదిగా ఒడ్డుకు చేరెను.

—the leaf gently reached the shore by the wind.

cheema prān̄anu rakshimpabadenu.
చీమ ప్రాణము రక్షింపబడెను.

—The life of the ant was saved.

mari yokanādu oka vētakādu pāvuramunu guri
మరి యొకనాడు ఒక వేటగాడు పావురమును గురి

C̄hoochi kottanundenu.
చూచి కొట్టనుండెను.

—another day, a hunter was about to shoot the pigeon.

cheema ad̄i C̄hoochenu.
చీమ అది చూచెను—the ant saw it.

ventanē ad̄i vāni kālu kar̄achenu.
వెంటనే అది వాని కాలు కఱచెను.

—immediately, it bit his leg.

anduvalana vētakāni guri thappi pōyenu.
అందువలన వేటకాని గురి తప్పి పోయెను.

—thereby, the hunter missed his aim.

pāvuramu egiri pōyenu.
పావురము ఎగిరి పోయెను—the pigeon flew away.

dāni prāṇamu rakshimpa badenu.
దాని ప్రాణము రక్షింప బడెను.

—its life was saved.

itlu cheema, pāvuramu thama snēhithamuchē
ఇట్లు చీమ పావురము తమ స్నేహితముచే

okadāni prāṇamu mariyokati kāpādi galiginavi.
ఒకదాని ప్రాణము మరియొకటి కాపాడ గలిగినవి.

—thus, the ant and the pigeon were able to save each other's life by their friendship.

Kashtarjithamu
కష్టార్జితము

Hard-earned money

oka bhāgyavanthunaku oka kumārudu undenu.
ఒక భాగ్యవంతునకు ఒక కుమారుడు ఉండెను.

—A rich man had a son.

ā pillavādu dhanamunu anavasaramugā vyayamu-
ఆ పిల్లవాడు ధనమును అనవసరముగా వ్యయము

chēyuchundenu
చేయుచుండెను.

—that boy was spending money unnecessarily.

pillavāni manassunu mārchavalenani thandri enthō
పిల్లవాని మనస్సును మార్చవలెనని తండ్రి ఎంతో

prayathninchenu.
ప్రయత్నించెను.

—The father tried much to change his son's mind.

kāni athani prayathnamanthayu vrudhā ayyenu.
కాని అతని ప్రయత్నమంతయు వృథా అయ్యెను.

—But all his efforts were in vain.

chivaraku athaniki oka upāyamu thattenu.
చివరకు అతనికి ఒక ఉపాయము తట్టెను.

—He hit upon a plan at last.

athadu thana kumāruni pilichi itlu cheppenu.
అతడు తన కుమారుని పిలిచి ఇట్లు చెప్పెను.

—He called his son and told him thus.

nāyanā, neevu etlayinanu nālugu aṇālu sampā-
"నాయనా, నీవు ఎట్లయినను నాలుగు అణాలు సంపా

dinchi thechchina chō, nēnu neeku nā āsthi anthayu
దించి తెచ్చిన చో, నేను నీకు నా ఆస్తి అంతయు

ichchi vēsedanu.
ఇచ్చి వేసెదను."

—"my dear son, if you will however earn and get four annas, I will give you all my property."

kumārudu "sare" ani oorilōniki pōyi nālugu aṇālu
కుమారుడు "సరె" అని ఊరిలోనికి పోయి నాలుగు అణాలు

sampādinchutakī enthō prayathninchenu,
సంపాదించుటకై ఎంతో ప్రయత్నించెను.

—The son agreed, went into the village and tried to earn four annas.

chāla kashtamu meeda athadu oka kammari vāni
చాల కష్టము మీద అతడు ఒక కమ్మరి వాని

vadda rōju anthayu kooli chēsi nālugu aṇālu sampā-
వద్ద రోజు అంతయు కూలి చేసి నాలుగు అణాలు సంపా

dimpa galigenu.
దింప గలిగెను.

—with great difficulty, he could earn four annas by toiling for the whole day under a Blacksmith.

appudu athaniki dhanamu sampādinchuta entha
అప్పుడు అతనికి ధనము సంపాదించుట ఎంత

kashtamō thelisenu.
కష్టమో తెలిసెను.

—Then he understood how difficult it is to earn money.

ventanē athadu thana thandrivaddaku pōyi āyana
వెంటనే అతడు తన తండ్రివద్దకు పోయి ఆయన

kāllapī padi, jarigina sangathi cheppi, kshamimpumu ani
కాళ్లపై పడి, జరిగిన సంగతి చెప్పి, క్షమింపుము అని

prārthinchenu.
ప్రార్థించెను.

—Immediately he went to his father, fell on his feet, and having told him what had happened, he requested him to forgive him.

thana kumāruni manassu māriananduku thandri
తన కుమారుని మనస్సు మారినందుకు తండ్రి

migula santhōshinchenu.
మిగుల సంతోషించెను.

—The father was very glad that his son's mind took a favourable turn.

anubhavamunu minchina guruvu lēdu
అనుభవమును మించిన గురువు లేదు

—There is no better teacher than experience.

kōthi—pillulu
కోతి—పిల్లులు

The monkey and the Cats.

okanādu rendu pillulaku oka rottemukka dorakenu.
ఒకనాడు రెండు పిల్లులకు ఒక రొట్టెముక్క దొరకెను.

—One day two cats found a piece of bread.

avi ā rottemukkanu thamalō thāmu panchukonalēka
అవి ఆ రొట్టెముక్కను తమలో తాము పంచుకొనలేక

pōyinavi.
పోయినవి.

—They could not divide that piece of bread between them.

anduchē avi rendunu okadānithō okati pōrādukona
అందుచే అవి రెండును ఒకదానితో ఒకటి పోరాడుకొన

sāgenu.
సాగెను.

—They, therefore, began to quarrel with each other.

appudu oka kōthi akkadaku vachchi pillulanu
అప్పుడు ఒక కోతి అక్కడకు వచ్చి పిల్లులను

"sangathi ēmi" ani adigenu.
"సంగతి ఏమి" అని అడిగెను.

—Then, a monkey came there and asked the cats what the matter was.

ā pillulu kōthiki jarigina sangathini cheppi thamaku
ఆ పిల్లులు కోతికి జరిగిన సంగతిని చెప్పి తమకు

nyāyamu kalugajēyavalenu ani dānini kōrinavi.
న్యాయము కలుగజేయవలెను అని దానిని కోరినవి.

—The cats told the monkey what had happened and requested it to do justice to them.

anthata ā kōthi ā rottemukkanu theesikoni rendugā
అంతట ఆ కోతి ఆ రొట్టెముక్కను తీసుకొని రెండుగా

virichi, oka thrāsulō ā rendu mukkalanu vēsi thoochenu.
విరిచి, ఒక త్రాసులో ఆ రెండు ముక్కలను వేసి తూచెను.

—Then, the monkey took that piece of bread and breaking it into two pieces, weighed them in a balance.

oka mukka rendava mukkakante konchemu baruvugā
ఒక ముక్క రెండవ ముక్కకంటె కొంచెము బరువుగా

undenu.
ఉండెను.

—one piece was a little heavier than the other.

kābatti, kōthi baruvugā unna mukkanu thrāsu nundi
కాబట్టి, కోతి బరువుగా ఉన్న ముక్కను త్రాసు నుండి

theesi konchemu kor̄iki, marala thrāsulō petti thoochenu.
తీసి కొంచెము కొఱికి, మరల త్రాసులో పెట్టి తూచెను.

—therefore, the monkey took out the heavier piece from the balance and biting off a little bit from it, replaced it in the balance.

ippudu rendava mukka konchemu baruvugā unnadi
ఇప్పుడు రెండవ ముక్క కొంచెము బరువుగా ఉన్నది

—now, the second piece is a little heavier (than the first.)

kōthi ā rendava mukkanu theesi konchemu kor̄iki
కోతి ఆ రెండవ ముక్కను తీసి కొంచెము కొఱికి

thrāsulō pettenu.
త్రాసులో పెట్టెను.

—The monkey took the second piece and replaced it in the balance after bitting a bit off it.

itlu ā kōthi ā rendu mukkalanu samānamīnavigā chēyu
ఇట్లు ఆ కోతి ఆ రెండు ముక్కలను సమానమైనవిగా చేయు

takī kor̄iki kor̄iki chinnavigā chēsenu.
టకై కొఱికి కొఱికి చిన్నవిగా చేసెను.

pillulu thāmu chēsina paniki paschāththāpapadi ā
పిల్లులు తాము చేసిన పనికి పశ్చాత్తాపపడి ఆ

migilina mukkalanu thamaku ichchivēyavalenani kōthini
మిగిలిన ముక్కలను తమకు ఇచ్చివేయవలెనని కోతిని

kōrenu.
కోరెను.

—The cats repented for their action and requested the monkey to give back the remaining pieces to them.

â kōthi, "nēnu meekoṟaku enthō śrama padināānu
ఆ కోతి "నేను మీకొఱకు ఎంతో శ్రమ పడినాను

käbatti ee migilina mukkalu nēnē theesikondunu" ani
కాబట్టి ఈ మిగిలిన ముక్కలు నేనే తీసికొందును" అని

cheppi, vānini thinuchu pōyenu.
చెప్పి, వానిని తినుచు పోయెను.

—The monkey said, 'I have taken so much trouble for you. Therefore, I will take these remaining pieces (of bread) for myself,' and it went away eating them.

neethi :— cheddavārini chēradeeyarādu.
నీతి :— చెడ్డవారిని చేరదీయరాదు.

—Bad people should be kept afar.